ORIENTEERING ME

AND GPS TECHNOLOGY

AN INSTRUCTIONAL HANDBOOK

Nancy Kelly

authorHOUSE®

AuthorHouse™ LLC
1663 Liberty Drive
Bloomington, IN 47403
www.authorhouse.com
Phone: 1-800-839-8640

Published by AuthorHouse   09/26/2014

ISBN: 978-1-4772-4859-1 (sc)
ISBN: 978-1-4772-4860-7 (e)

Library of Congress Control Number: 2012913014

PART ONE

ORIENTEERING
MADE SIMPLE

By Nancy Kelly

PART ONE ORIENTEERING
TABLE OF CONTENTS

SECTION ONE FIRST STEPS IN ORIENTEERING INDOOR MAP SKILLS

SECTION TWO OUTDOOR MAP SKILLS

SECTION THREE INTERMEDIATE ORIENTEERING USING A COMPASS

MAP ADVENTURE PROGRAMS

Orienteering is a sport that is all about maps. It can be enjoyed by people of all ages, either as a recreational activity or as a competitive sport. This book is designed to introduce orienteering to school students as well as youth organizations of all ages.

MULTIDISCIPLINARY APPROACH

In a carefully designed step-by-step process, participants learn to navigate first in a classroom, then in a schoolyard or park, and finally in the forest at a regular orienteering meet. The entire process is one that fosters:

SELF CONFIDENCE   **COOPERATIVE LEARNING**

PROBLEM SOLVING   **TEAM BUILDING**

DECISION-MAKING   **LOVE FOR THE OUTDOORS**

Programs are easily adaptable to a wide variety of grade levels and can be designed to enhance most subject areas. Below is a sampling of concepts and skills that can be experienced through orienteering and orienteering maps.

PERSONAL DEVELOPMENT
Self-esteem
Problem Solving
Self-confidence
Team building
Organizational skills
Responsibility
Concentration
Social relationships
Memory skills
Decision making

SCIENCE
Magnetism
Contour interpretation
Land forms
Habitat analysis
Compass usage
Ecology

ART
Observation
Drawing
Perspective
Visualization

PHYSICAL EDUCATION
Aerobic activity
Lifetime sports
Skill assessment
Cooperative learning
Personal health

SOCIAL STUDIES
Exploring
New environments
Map legends
Handling skills
Grids
Land usage

MATH
Estimating
Word problems
Mental computation
Calculating
Metric system
Real life application
Pacing
Spatial relationships
Precision

LANGUAGE ARTS
Comprehension Writing directions
Writing about experiences
Listening

TECHNOLOGY
Surveying
Computer drawing
Internet communications
Software application

TYPES OF ORIENTEERING

Orienteering courses can be set in any environment where an appropriate map has been made.

STRING ORIENTEERING: Often used with preschoolers and primary grade children. Controls are placed along a string, which leads the child to each of the controls.

STAR ORIENTEERING: Participants must return to start between each control. Used mainly for training.

MOTALA (individual or group relay): Excellent for schoolyards and small areas. Participants do a loop of several controls and return to the start.

TRIVIA ORIENTEERING: Proof of arrival at each control site is confirmed by answering a question about the site.

MYSTERY ORIENTEERING: Maps are marked indicating controls to be located. Participants mark off clues on their scorecard when they find the control with the clue on it. This is an excellent training event for improving map-reading skills.

LINE ORIENTEERING: Maps are marked with a line indicating the exact route to be followed. Participants mark their map where they find each control. Good for beginner map reading skill training.

PROJECT ORIENTEERING: At each control the participants attempt to complete some type of activity. The activity may be used to teach a new concept or used to test a skill.

CROSS COUNTRY (point to point): A course of controls to be taken in a specific order is laid out. Lengths vary from a few kilometers for beginners to ten or more kilometers for experts. This is a classic form of orienteering.

SCORE ORIENTEERING: Participants try to find as many controls as possible in a given amount of time. Controls usually have different point values depending upon distance from the start and the difficulty of control placement.

Other types of orienteering are:

- Bike orienteering
- Canoe orienteering
- Ski orienteering
- Trail orienteering- designed for those with disabilities

MULTIDISCIPLINARY TECHNIQUES TAUGHT THROUGH MAP ADVENTURES

COURSE DESCRIPTION

Orienteering is a lifetime activity in which the participant uses a detailed map to develop strategies on how to navigate to a series of locations. Orienteering is both a competitive and recreational sport with a number of concepts and skills that can easily be integrated into the classroom. Through adaptations of orienteering, students can explore new areas of learning in many different subject areas. This exciting addition to any curriculum can be modified for preschool through college age. The skills of orienteering also apply to everyday navigation with a variety of maps. Orienteering is an excellent vehicle for developing problem solving, decision-making, cooperative learning, and improving self-esteem.

COURSE OUTLINE

Goals: Through a series of hands-on activities, participants will learn about orienteering and explore the many ways orienteering can be incorporated into their school programs using a multidisciplinary teaching approach.

Objectives:

1 The learner will become familiar with orienteering as a sport and teaching technique.
2 The learner will identify the types of orienteering.
3 The learner will develop basic orienteering techniques.
4 The learner will use these techniques to teach orienteering.
5 The learner will develop activities to incorporate orienteering into his/her current school program.
6 The learner will be introduced to orienteering materials and resources.
7 The learner will learn how to make simple orienteering maps.
8 The learner will design and set up an orienteering course.
9 The learner will explore ways orienteering can be used to develop self-confidences and decision-making.
10 The learner will discover ways orienteering can be used as a cooperative learning activity.
11 The learner will develop navigational and map handling skills.
12 The learner will have opportunities to enhance problem-solving skills.

Section One

First Steps in Orienteering

Indoor Map Skills

INTRODUCTION TO ORIENTEERING

THE EVENT

In orienteering participants receive a map of an area that shows a series of sites. Participants develop strategies, which they use to navigate to locate these sites. It is a sport that can be done both competitively and for fun. It blends both mental and physical activity. It is often referred to as **THE THINKING SPORT** or **CUNNING RUNNING**.

Orienteering can begin in a small area like a classroom and everything in the room is very specific; example, top right corner versus top left corner, or bottom right and left corners are important when locating clues. All little features within the room must be taken into consideration when trying to locate control sites. As the area gets larger, smaller details become less important. For example when you move from a room to a building the details in the room are not important other than the fact that they may have a closet in them. What becomes more important is the room itself in relationship to other rooms and fixtures in the building. Once you progress to an area outside a building which includes surrounding fields and other building structures, the interior of any area are no longer significant, but outside structures and alleys, roads, and other details relevant to the outside surroundings become important. When the area gets even larger specific details surrounding a particular building or site might become less significant. Things that take on more significance would be roads, trails, streams, bridges, and cliffs, etc., which may become important as handrails for finding where you are going. The greater the distance covered the more general the entire picture becomes and the smaller the area the more specific every detail becomes.

ANTICIPATED OUTCOME

- Sketch maps of simple inside and outside areas
- Have a basic understanding of orienteering symbols
- Interpret map features
- Thumb an orienteering map
- Make good route choice decisions

ACTIVITY ONE

How well can you remember objects that you have seen? Try this simple exercise. Have everyone close their eyes and ask them specific questions about the room they are in. How many details can they remember? What was written on the chalk board? Is there a clock in the room and if so where is it? What was on the front right hand corner of the desk? You may go to a different room so the students are not tempted to open their eyes and cheat.

PRE-LESSON DISCUSSION

The following topics should be discussed with the group before beginning the Orienteering Unit.

Brainstorm

What is orienteering?

- Orienteering is navigating one's way through known or unknown terrain with the use of a special map and sometimes a compass.
- Orienteering is both a recreational and an elite sport.
- Orienteering experiences may include any map reading experience such as consulting a street map, a mall directory, or a map of bus routes.
- Orienteering may be experienced in different ways (ski's, running, walking).

Discussion

What is a map? Discuss the different types of maps and what their purposes are.

- A map is a reduced picture of the ground from a bird's eye view. It is a 2 dimensional (or flat) graphic representation of a 3 dimensional world.
- Maps have been created to help people visualize areas before they see them.
- Many types of maps exist; road, topographic (relief), world, directory, transportation, hiking, architecture, tourist, town, and city.
- Maps usually have a title, a scale (for distance calculations), a North directional arrow, a legend (explaining the symbols and colors used on the map) and topic specific detail (hiking trails, vegetation, city plans, etc.).
- Some maps use international symbols and standards so that they can be used throughout the world and by people of many different languages.
- An orienteering map differs from other maps in the following way:
  1. More detail including features such as boulders, small depressions, trails, and vegetation boundaries.
  2. A large scale of a smaller area than most topographic maps.
  3. A magnetic north orientation rather than a true north orientation (eliminating the need to account for magnetic declination)
  4. All symbols and colors are of International Orienteering Federation specifications.

Discuss the various types of orienteering

Because orienteering requires mainly map reading, the type of physical activity may vary: running, walking, canoeing, cycling, skiing, or snowshoeing. Other variations include 24-hour events, and the ever-popular Scandinavian event- night orienteering with headlamps.

Orienting a map by inspection:

Keeping the map oriented is a critical skill in orienteering. The map is oriented when the map features are matched up directionally with the terrain and with the surrounding features.

START   **FINISH**   **START/FINISH**

The start location symbol is represented by a triangle, a double circle represents the finish location symbol, and a common start/finish is represented by a triangle inside a circle.

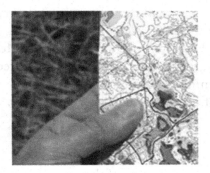

Holding, Folding, and "Thumbing"

Once the map is oriented, fold the map with one fold so that the area where the orienteer is and where the orienteer is going is exposed. Hold the map (usually held in the left hand), in the crux of the index finger and thumb, with the thumb on the top surface of the map and the other fingers underneath to give it a "table-like" stability. The orienteer's thumb should be placed on the starting location and then should "follow" along on the main features on the map as they are passed in the terrain.

Map Symbols:

Map symbols are graphic representations on a map of features in the terrain. For example a large solid black dot is the symbol for a boulder. (All the symbols are in the materials supplement).

LESSON ONE
THEME: POINT-TO-POINT ORIENTEERING

OBJECTIVE: To practice locating their position on a map.
To find control points using a large-scale map.

MATERIALS

- Indoor area with distinct features (doors, tables, chairs, etc.)
- Large scale map of room
- Set of control cards and pencils

PREPARATION

1. Create simple features in the room
2. Plan 12—15 control sites.
3. Mark all the control sites on all the maps with red circles
4. Mark the start/finish with a triangle
5. Create control codes. Each control code identifies a different control. Control codes can be anything you want them to be. For example, selected letters can be unscrambled to create a phrase "Cunning Running"
6. Create the number of controls needed for the activity.

ACTIVITY

1. Evaluate the group's understanding of the map and the symbols used. Look at the large map and ask individual children to identify specific features in the room.
2. Show the group a sample control and how it is going to be symbolized on the map. Discuss that the map is not 3 dimensional and indicate the height range and where the control may be located.
3. Set the map so it is orientated to the room on the floor so everyone can see it.
4. On the map, find the control with number "1" beside it. This is the first control. Walk around the set map until you are looking in the direction of the control as viewed from the start. Pick up the map. The map is set.
5. Go to control 1 and mark down the letter found on the control card. Continue to control 2, 3, etc. until all the controls have been visited.

The game card is in the materials supplement at the end of the book.

POINT TO POINT ORIENTEERING

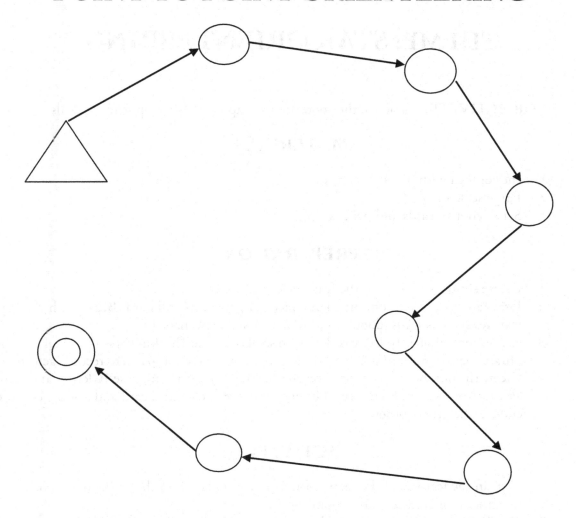

Start at the triangle and follow the lines from one control point to the next until your reach the finish, which is indicated by the double circle.

LESSON TWO
THEME: STAR ORIENTEERING

OBJECTIVE: To introduce the concept of a map and basic map reading skills.

MATERIALS

- Indoor area with distinct features
- Large scale map
- Set of control cards and pencils

PREPARATION

1 Create simple symbols for the features in the room.
2 Draw a map of the room on a large piece of paper or cardboard. Begin with the key features such as walls, doors, windows, chairs, tables, mats, etc.
3 Create control sites. In this case letters to spell out "The Thinking Sport". When using a phrase the control card will have the appropriate number of spaces to record each code.
4 Create the number of controls necessary for the activity. In this case 16 letters and thus 16 controls. Number the control in one corner of the control card and put the control code in the other corner.

ACTIVITY

1 Explain the features of the map to the group and place it in the center of the room on the ground orientated to the room.
2 Hand out the control cards and have them put their names on their cards.
3 Explain to them that they should:
   - Read the map carefully
   - Find all the controls in any order
   - Record the control code in the appropriate numbered box by matching the number of the control to the numbered box on their control card
   - Work individually and try not to give away the location of a control
   - Unscramble the coded phrase

4   Encourage everyone to return to the center map frequently to check locations
5   Continue until the majority of the group have completed the course and have unscrambled the coded phrase.
6   For more advanced groups try this variation. Place additional false letters scattered around the room forcing the students to focus more on clear map reading skills.

Time permitting let everyone try to draw a map of the room.

DISCUSSION

Get the group together and go over the activity.

- How did they manage to find out where they were on the map- map/self-orientation?
- What was their process of finding the control?
- Which controls were easiest/hardest to find and why?
- Which room features help to read the map?
- What decisions had to be made to find the correct controls?
- Was it difficult trying to draw a 2-dimensional map from the 3-dimensional room?

The game card is in the materials supplement at the end of the book.

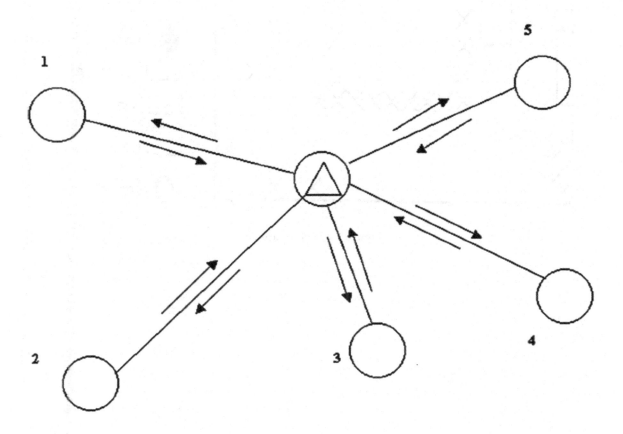

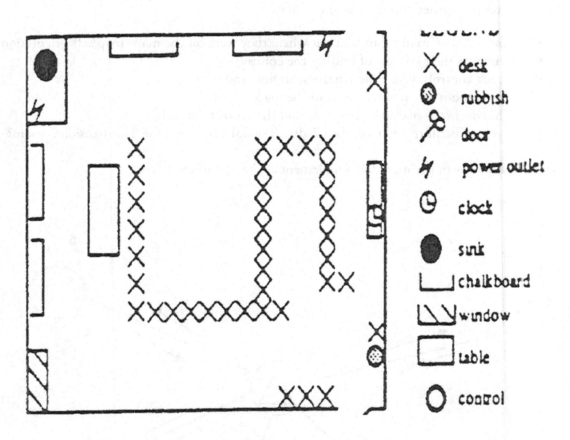

Figure 1 drawing sample

LESSON THREE
THEME: MOTALA ORIENTEERING

OBJECTIVE: To practice locating control points as a group.

MATERIALS

- Master map of indoor area
- Set of small maps
- Set of control cards and pencils

PREPARATION

1 Plan a variety of control locations; easy and difficult and long and short distances from the start location. Mark them on the master map in a random or non-sequential manner.
2 Have the students mark all the control sites on their maps with a colored pencil.
3 Mark the start/finish with a triangle.
4 Create 3 or more different courses.
5 Create control codes. In this case the control codes are puzzle pieces.
6 Create the number of control sites needed for the activity.

ACTIVITY

Motala orienteering involves using 3 or more different courses and they can be done in any order.

Divide the group into 2 teams. Give each team a master map with 12 control sites that they must transcribe onto their own maps.

1 Have the team decide how best to split up the group. This involves team cooperation and planning to figure out who are the quickest as well as the best at navigating.
2 The teams are competing for time to see which team can complete the puzzle first. The teams can use whatever strategy they like to achieve their goal. Everyone in the group must be involved.
3 Try to divide the control sites evenly amongst the members in the team so that each group is trying to locate 3 or 4 control points (puzzle pieces).

4   When each team and group has his or her respective maps, give the signal to start the competition.

5   Go to only the control points on your map and pick up the puzzle piece at the control site.

6   The first team to complete the puzzle wins.

MOTALA ORIENTEERING

There are 3 different courses with three or four control points for each course. All have the same start and stop point.

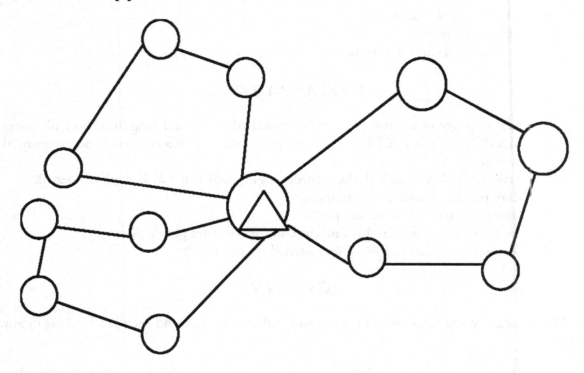

LESSON FOUR
THEME: MYSTERY ORIENTEERING

OBJECTIVE: Reinforce individual map skills while competing in a "Who don' it" game.

MATERIALS

- Master maps of area with different starting points
- Set of small maps
- Set of control cards and pencils

PREPARATION

1 Plan a variety of control locationus, easy and difficult throughout the building using building features (doorways, halls, fire escapes, etc.) Mark them on the master map in a random or non-sequential manner.
2 Have the students mark all the control sites on their maps with a colored pencil.
3 Have the class work in a group of 2 or 3 or individually.
4 Mark the start with a triangle. There are 8 to 10 master maps with different starting points.
5 Create control codes. In this case the control codes are clues to a mystery.
6 Create the number of control sites needed for the activity.

ACTIVITY

The scene is set. Someone has found a dead body, but nobody knows where it happened, by whom, or how they were killed (like the game of "CLUE").

1 Give everyone a game card (control card) with the list of possible suspects, weapons that may have been used, and a list of rooms or areas where the crime occurred. The task is to locate the clues and solve the mystery. The clues are scattered around the building.
2 Everyone is given one of the 8 master maps. They are to transcribe all the control points from the master and the starting point onto their individual map.

3   The first task is to locate the starting point, which will tell them what color game card they are to use. Having different starting points will encourage random searching and discourage teams following each other.

4   All the control points must be located in order to find the solution.

5   Everyone must be able to read a map and navigate his or her way through the building.

6   The control sites can be visited in random order.

7   All of the control sites give clues to solve the mystery.

8   There is a random start but the finish is dependent upon finding all the clues.

9   The first person or team to find all the clues and solve the mystery wins.

DISCUSSION

Were the clues easy or hard to find? Did you find yourself following other teams or did you stay independent of everyone? Did you try to guess the answer before you found all of the clues? Did you have fun? Would you have used a different way to start the exercise or did this way of starting work? Did you need help finding some of the clues? Do you think you could now read an outdoor map and continue to practice orienting the map and thumbing the map?

MYSTERY "O"

Name: _____ Class Period: _____

SUSPECTS	found
Ms. Tisdale	
Mrs. Snow	
Dr. Pipps	
Mr. Brown	
Mr. Parker	
WEAPONS	
Revolver	
Tire Wrench	
Rope	
Dumb Bell	
Knife	
ROOMS	
Auditorium	
Garage	
Hall	
Lounge	
Study	
Kitchen	
Dining Room	
Court Yard	
Elevator	
Laboratory	
Library	

Color Codes			
Green	Red	Orange	Purple
Yellow	Blue	Black	Black

Section Two

Outdoor Map Skills

SECTION TWO

In order to progress to the next level of orienteering it will be necessary to build on the knowledge and skills from Section One and begin to use larger, more detailed outdoor maps. At this point you will need to be able to:

- Sketch maps of simple outside areas and use symbols to represent features
- Practice folding, holding and thumbing a map
- Relate the map to actual features on the ground
- Recognize map symbols used on the map as graphic representations of features in the terrain
- Orient the map features directionally with the terrain and surrounding features
- Understand how to make route choice decisions
- Challenge map reading skills in a competitive timed activity
- Develop team work and good sportsmanship

ORIENTEERING SYMBOLS

In order to be successful in orienteering it is important to be able to read a map and recognize the different symbols that are used in orienteering. There are a few different activities that you can do with the class to help them learn the symbols and to have fun in the process.

ACTIVITY ONE

Have everyone practice the symbols by using flash cards. Go over the flash cards two times as a group and then try to have the student's name the symbols as you go through the cards a third time. Some groups may be able to do it on the second try.

Play a game of ROUND UP. Place all of the symbols on the ground. Divide the class into two teams. Have the teams stand behind a designated line as you scatter all the symbols on the ground. There should be two complete sets of symbols, one for each team. The first person in each team is given a name of a symbol to find. Their task is to go and retrieve the symbol and bring that card back and give it to the next person on their team who must retrieve the symbol that is written on the back of the first card. This sequence will be followed until all the cards are collected. This can only be done if the cards are picked up in the correct sequence so that the last card that is picked up is blank on the reverse side and all the symbols have been collected.

Set UP: To prepare for this activity you will need to use the symbols found in the material supplement. The first card says START on one side and the word of a symbol on the reverse side. When you find the picture of the symbol the reverse side of that card will indicate the next symbol to find in the game sequence. Set all the cards up this way. The last card might say "Congratulations you WON" on the reverse side. There is only one solution to this game and if the last card is picked before all the cards are pick up it will be necessary to back track to try to correct the problem. Try to encourage teamwork to solve the problem and win the game.

ACTIVITY TWO

This involves a handout where symbols are drawn in a story and the fun is in trying to decipher the story by putting the name of the symbol into the story where indicated. An example is A WALK IN THE WOODS.

ACTIVITY THREE

Give everyone in the class a piece of graph paper, which they will use to draw their own map. This map drawing activity will reinforce the understanding of map symbols, cardinal directions, and distance. Students are given the outline of an island in an ocean, N, S, E, and W references are shown on the edges of the map. They will receive directions telling them where to draw in certain symbols on the map. The name of this activity is called MAPPING FANTASY ISLAND. The more advanced the class the more map symbols can be used.

A WALK IN THE WOODS

Once upon a time there were three students who decided to go for a walk in the woods.

They left their ■ and had to cross the ⋯⋅⋅ . They passed many ⬆

and 🌳 as they walked along the ——— .They followed a ∼∼

which eventually brought them to a ∠ . They traveled on the – – – – – which came

to a ▬ . The only way they could get across was by going over a ⋈ . Once they

got to the other side of the ▬ , they came to a —•—•— . They went through and

came upon a ⌐⌐ . Inside the ⌐⌐ there were ⌐¬ and ⊤

, but they were not in good condition. There were also many large ● which must

have come from the ⌐⊤⊤⊤ that was on the North side of the ⌐⌐ . They

decided to keep going because it was starting to get dark and there were no ✦

.

They had to climb a ⬭ but at the bottom they came to an ⬯ so they

had to try to go around it. They were beginning to think they would never get out of the

woods when they came upon a ═══════ . They saw a ⊙ and they

realized they were almost home.

ACTIVITY THREE

MAPPING FANTASY ISLAND

- Start out drawing a large island on a piece of graph and mark N., S., E., & W. Each box of the graph paper will measure one mile for distance purposes only.
- A trail starts at the NW corner of the island and goes S 8 miles until it comes to a cliff. The trail turns E and travels along the top of the cliff for 3 miles until it reaches a stream.
- A trail goes across the stream and continues E for 10 miles until it comes to a ruin. The ruin has 4 large boulders around it.
- South of the ruin a stone wall travels S for 12 miles until it meets a dirt road. The dirt road continues E until it comes to the shore where there is a light pole. Power lines run from the light pole to the factory.
- A main road starts from the light pole and travels SW for 13 miles.
- At the 9 mile marker there is a bridge that crosses over a lake. At the end of the main road there is a sign that says SHARP TURN SLOW DOWN.
- The road makes a sharp turn and travels NW for 13 miles until it comes to a dirt road.
- The dirt road travels W for 5 miles until it comes to a school building. There is a parking lot on the NE side of the building.
- A flagpole is just south of the building.
- On the W side of the school is a large field with soccer goals at each end. There are lights around the playing field and a score board at the NE corner. There are also bleachers along the west side of the field.
- S of the soccer field is a playground with various playground equipment.
- A vegetation boundary runs along the W and S sides of the playground.
- There is root stock beyond the vegetation boundary along with a sewer system.

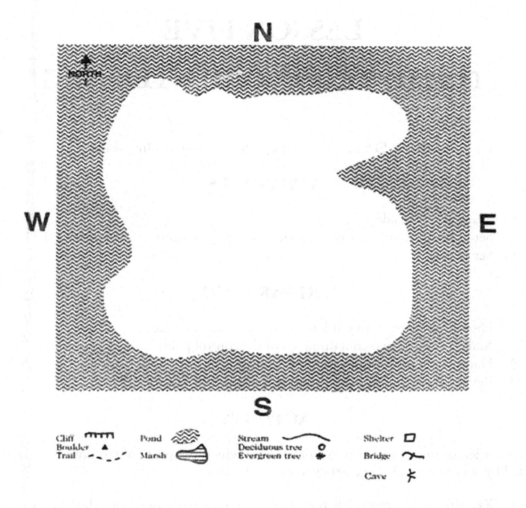

Cliff ⊓⊓⊓	Pond 〰	Stream ⌒	Shelter ▭
Boulder ▲		Deciduous tree ○	
Trail -·-·-	Marsh	Evergreen tree ♣	Bridge
			Cave ⅄

Go through the instructions several times so that the students understand the process. A variation of this activity can be used. More or fewer map symbols can be used, especially simple terrain features (depression, pit, knoll, hill, and gully). Also, color can be used to show features as well: BLACK for man-made features and rock features; BROWN for contour features like hills, knolls, depressions, etc.; BLUE for water, marsh, stream, lake, etc.; GREEN for thick forest; YELLOW for open areas like a field or meadow.

LESSON FIVE
THEME: TRIVIA ORIENTEERING

OBJECTIVE: To encourage outdoor map reading skills.

MATERIALS

- Maps of an outside area
- Set of blank control cards to answer the trivia questions at each control site
- Set of pencils

PREPARATION

1 Photocopy maps of an outdoor area containing a legend.
2 Make a master map containing all of the control points circled.
3 Hand out copies of the master trivia answer sheet.
4 Review symbols, handrails, attack points, and collecting features.

ACTIVITY

Trivia orienteering is a form of orienteering in which the proof of visitation to a control is provided by answering a trivia question about the location.

1 Explain to the group that they are looking for trivia questions that correspond to a control location.
2 Give everyone an outdoor map and have him or her transcribe all of the control sites onto their maps.
3 The control sites can be visited in any order. If you find the control site but cannot answer the question, write the question in the appropriate box.
4 Each control site will have a number and a question next to it. Make sure you put the correct answer next to the proper number on the control card.

TRIVIA ORIENTEERING SAMPLE SHEET

Trivia Orienteering Question Sheet

#	Trivia Question	Answer
1.	Name a state that starts and ends in the same letter.	
2.	Another name for twelve dozen?	
3.	Name a month with only 30 days.	

Master Trivia Orienteering Answer Sheet

#	Trivia Question	Answer
1.	Name a state that starts and ends in the same letter.	Ohio
2.	Another name for 1twelve dozen?	Gross
3.	Name a month with only 30 days.	June

Game card is in the material supplement at the end of the book.

LESSON SIX
THEME: PROJECT ORIENTEERING

OBJECTIVE: To challenge map reading abilities and to encourage sportsmanlike behavior in a competitive, timed activity.

MATERIALS

- Master map with clearly defined boundaries
- Set of sample maps to be transcribed onto
- 10-15 controls with a description of the project at every station
- Stop watch

PREPARATION

1   Plan a variety of control locations; easy and difficult; and short and long distances from the start location. Mark them on the master maps in a random or non-sequential manner for the students to copy from.
2   Assign a task or project at each control.
3   Secure control descriptions and control cards at each of the locations.
4   Place all the equipment necessary to complete the task at each of the controls.

ACTIVITY

1   Hand out blank maps and have the students copy the control locations onto their own map.
2   Explain that there is a stunt or task to do at each of the control sites and proof of arrival at a control site will depend upon their group completing the task.
3   Explain that each member of the group should plan a strategy for locating the control point in the least amount of time and making sure that they can complete the task.
4   The controls may be found in any order.
5   Stress group navigation.
6   Explain that there will be bonus points added to their team's score by not exceeding the time limit as well as for completing the task at each of the controls they find.

7 Recommend that everyone studies the map and plans a strategy before taking off from the start.

8 Encourage participants to finish within the specified time. The whistle will indicate when time is up.

9 This activity can be done as a mass start or random start as long as each team receives a start time and the time lapse is calculated accordingly.

Sample course could include these projects:

1 Count how many steps you use to go 100 meters on the track (set up two markers to have them pace out).

2 Try to throw a tennis ball into a basket sitting on top of a basketball hoop.

3 Climb the bleachers and place a team marker on the top railing.

4 Assemble a simple puzzle.

5 Make a pyramid of blocks.

6 Hit a foam golf ball into a hoop.

7 Answer a riddle.

8 Collect a leaf and bring it with you.

Encourage team- work and good sportsmanship. Discourage cheating.

DISCUSSION

- Which controls were easy or difficult to locate?
- Did you use handrails, collecting features, and attack points for any of the controls?
- What were the effects of physical participation at the control sites?
- Which controls were the most popular/unpopular?
- Could you read your map while moving?
- Did you "thumb" your way along?
- Did the other groups distract you?

LESSON SEVEN
THEME: SCORE ORIENTEERING

OBJECTIVE: To encourage route choice strategies with a time constraint

MATERIALS

- Set of blank maps with clearly defined boundaries, such as roads, fences, or buildings
- Master maps
- 15-20 controls with codes and numbers
- Set of control cards
- Set of control descriptions and control point values
- Stop watch and whistle

PREPARATION

1 Plan a variety of control locations: easy and difficult; and short and long distances from the start location. Mark them on the map in a random or non-sequential manner.
2 Assign a point value for each control based on its level of difficulty and distance from the start.
3 Secure control cards to maps.
4 Assign a time limit, selecting a time that will allow most controls to be found, but not all of them.
5 Randomly number the controls on the map.
6 Set control.

ACTIVITY

This is one of the most versatile forms of Orienteering because it lends itself to any time frame, any size area, and will accommodate mass starting. It is also easy to organize. This exercise highlights the need to carefully select routes, which will cover as much terrain as possible within a specific time limit. The object is to collect as many points as possible within the time limit. Points are deducted for going overtime; for example, 5 points are deducted for every minute or part of a minute late.

1   Hand out maps and control cards. Copy the control locations from the master maps onto the blank maps.
2   Explain that this is a timed event and points are awarded for finding as many controls as possible within a time limit.
3   Recommend that everyone study the map and use strategy before taking off in order to find the most controls and the greatest number of points within the time period.
4   The controls may be found in any order.
5   Have the participants record the control code on their control card.
6   Explain that a whistle will blow when 4 minutes are left and that 2 long blows will indicate that time is up. Make sure that everyone understands the timing system and the importance of returning to the starting point before time elapses.
7   The start can be mass or random, but make sure everyone receives a start time and a finishing time and calculate accordingly.

POST ACTIVITY DISCUSSION

- Trade control cards with another team and calculate someone else's total points
- What strategies were used? What worked?
- What handrails, collecting features or other information were most helpful?
- What were the effects of physical and time limitations?

SCORE ORIENTEERING GAME CARD

Time Limit: 15 minutes
Penalty: 5 pts per minute late

Control #	Control Letter	Control Value	Control Description
1.			
2.			
3.			
4.			
5.			
6.			
7.			
8.			
9.			
10.			
11.			
12.			
13.			
14.			
15.			
16.			
17.			
18.			
19.			
20.			

Total Points	
Penalty Points	
Final Score	

LESSON EIGHT
THEME: TEAM RELAY ORIENTEERING

OBJECTIVE: To challenge map-reading abilities and encourage sportsmanship like behavior on a competitive, timed activity.

MATERIALS

- One map per team of 3-4
- Set of control cards
- One master control card
- 12 controls with codes and numbers
- Team Recorder Sheet

PREPARATION

1   Prepare 4 short courses (or more depending upon the number of teams) of 3-4 controls in a clover -leaf pattern with a common start/finish area.
2   Each course should only take 3-4 minutes to provide more active participation by everyone.
3   Have a master card with the proper controls for each course to cross check accuracy upon completion.
4   Teams should prepare their own maps from the master maps.
5   Set controls.

ACTIVITY

1   Have everyone on the team place their names on the control card.
2   Begin at the start/finish area and all team switches are to be made in this area.
3   Have each member carry the map with them to the control site and have them "follow" their way to the control on the map.
4   Make sure to mark the proper control code in the proper box on the control card.

Alternate variation allows the participants to set up the course.

Make this a three day event. The first day the students will form into three teams. Each team will be assigned an area of the fields around the school that they will set up their orienteering course on. They are to have 8 control sites (you may need to set up more or less depending upon the number of people on a team) that should be clearly defined on their maps. Make sure that they only mark clear boundaries (corner of fence, edge of building, goal posts, bleachers, sign posts, etc.).

Day Two the teams will go out and put the control markers at the control sites. Use the rip-away florescent caution tape that you can find at any hardware store (they come in different colors) to secure the cards at each location. It is a good idea to number each of the strips that are put out so they know that they picked up the right control marker. Give each team about 10-15 minutes to complete this task.

After this is done have the teams exchange maps with one of the other teams. On the signal (whistle) one team member from each team will go out to try to locate one of the controls. When they do they should run back give the map to another person on their team who will then try to locate another control site. Continue in this fashion until everyone on the team has gone out to get a control card or all 8 controls have been found. Record the time it takes each team to retrieve all 8 control markers.

Day Three will be just like day two but each team will take another team's map and try to locate the controls from that section of the field. Record the time it takes each team to retrieve all 8 control markers.

Calculate the two-day total to determine which team accomplished the task in the least amount of time.

*Note to teachers.
The transition site should be at one location and the person on the team who is retrieving the control card should carry the map with them to the control site. Each class will have their own set of maps and control cards which should be collected at the end of the period.

Section Three

Intermediate Orienteering

Using a Compass

READING A MAP

The ability to map read and to relate the map to the actual features on the ground is the basis of all orienteering and must be practiced constantly. The use of the compass in orienteering in conjunction with the map will develop a very high degree of skills.

In order to prepare for an official orienteering event it is essential to scaffold from acquired knowledge and to develop precise map reading skills as well as basic compass skills. The orienteer must make many decisions as to the best route to follow. This demands the ability to:

- Recognize features on the map
- Recognize directions on the map and know how to locate places based on their location to other objects or places around it.
- Become familiar with terminology used to read a map such as longitude and latitude, etc.
- Read fine contours and relate to actual landforms
- Judge actual distance in relation to map scale
- Learn how to estimate distances on a map by using step counting.
- Constantly relate the map to the ground to ensure accuracy in navigation
- Mentally tick off features as they are reached
- Become familiar with compass bearings and how to set ones bearings to locate places.

DIRECTIONAL AND COMPASS SKILLS

Compass Parts and Functions:

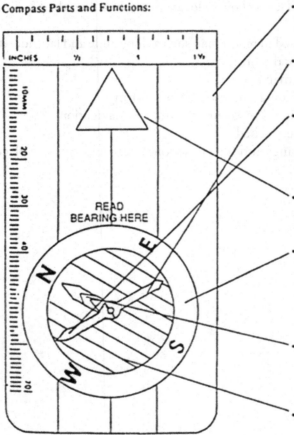

- **Base Plate:** the transparent surface which forms the base of the protractor baseplate compass. The direction-of-travel arrow and a measurement scale are engraved on it.

- **Magnetic Needle:** the flat red and white needle on a pivot in the middle of the housing. The red end of the needle will always rest pointing to magnetic north when held motionless in the horizontal plane.

- **Magnetic North:** the direction which the red end of the magnetic needle points to. The needle is affected by the earth's magnetic field and thus the red end of the magnetic needle will always point to magnetic north rather than true (geographic) north. All orienteering maps are drawn to magnetic north.

- **Direction-of-travel Arrow:** an engraved straight line which runs from the centre of the housing rim to the front edge of the base plate to indicate the direction of travel once the map and compass have been oriented.

- **Housing:** the round dial which contains the magnetic needle. The rim of the protractor compass housing rotates manually, identifies north and the other cardinal directions, and is divided into 360 degrees. The orienting arrow and parallel orienting lines are engraved on the base of the housing. The housing is filled with a fluid to help stabilize the magnetic needle.

- **Orienting Arrow:** engraved on the base of the compass housing and points directly to the housing's north marking. The compass is oriented when the red end of the magnetic needle is aligned with and is pointing in the same direction as the orienting arrow.

- **Orienting Lines:** engraved in the bottom of the housing and run parallel to the orienting arrow.

GOLD CHALLENGE - WRITTEN COMPONENT

Name: _____

COMPASS KNOWLEDGE

Correctly identify 5 compass parts by connecting the term with the part by drawing a line.

1. compass housing

2. direction-of-travel arrow

3. magnetic N needle

4. orienting arrow

5. magnetic north lines

6. measurement scale

Correctly match 5 compass functions.

7. orienting arrow

8. compass housing

9. magnetic needle

10. direction-of-travel arrow

11. measurement scale

12. orienting lines

_____ red end always points magnetic north

_____ engraved in the housing and runs parallel to north

_____ points to housing's north marking

_____ rotates to change bearing direction

_____ helps with measuring paces on the map

_____ followed once the map and compass are oriented

READING A MAP (1)

Study the map of the United States on Sheet 4 and try to answer correctly the following questions.

1. In what state do you live? _____

2. What is the capital of your state? _____

3. What states border your state? _____

4. Which states touch the Gulf of Mexico? _____

5. What ocean is east of the United States? _____

6. What ocean is west of the United States? _____

7. What country is north of the United States? _____

8. Which states touch the Pacific Ocean? _____

9. What state is south of South Dakota? _____

10. What state is north of New Mexico? _____

11. What country is south of Arizona? _____

12. Circle the names of any of the following states which are west of Illinois: California-Pennsylvania -West Virginia -Kansas -Louisiana -Maine Tennessee

13. Circle the names of any of the following states that do <u>NOT</u> touch the Great Lakes: New York - Indiana - Iowa - Minnesota - Vermont - New Jersey Michigan

*Use Reading a Map Worksheet

READING A MAP (2)

1. New York is located in the: NE, SE, SW, NW

   Texas is located in the: N, S, E, W

2. Find a four (4) letter state in the west? _____

3. What state is the most NW? _____

4. What state is the most NE? _____

5. What state is the most SE? _____

6. What state is the most SW? _____

7. What state is 100° longitude and 40° latitude? _____

8. What is at 30° latitude and 80° longitude? _____

9. What degree latitude and longitude do you live in? _____

10. What degree latitude and longitude is Nevada? _____

11. How far is it from New York to California? _____

12. How far is it from Delaware to Nebraska? _____

13. If you travel 600 miles west of Iowa where will you be? _____

*Use Reading a Map Worksheet

READING A MAP   (Sheet 4)

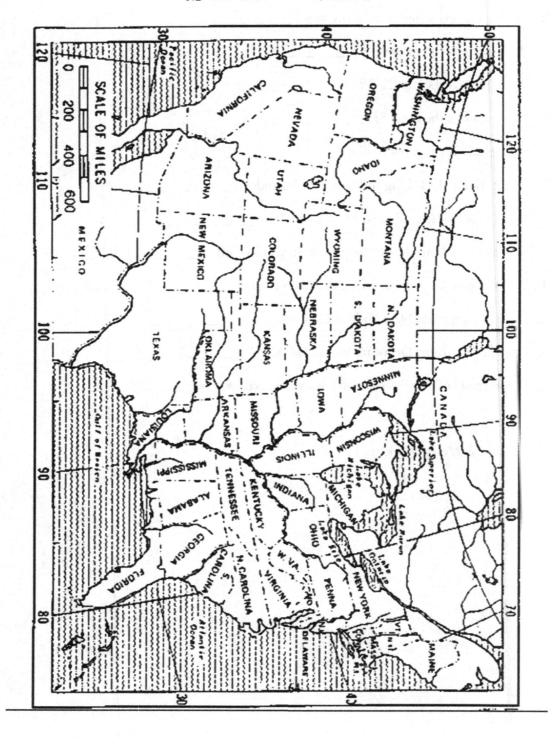

SCALE AND DISTANCE

Maps are, by necessity, drawn to scale and it is this scale, which determines the distance between points on the actual ground.

SCALE

The scale of the map indicates the distance between points shown on the map. At a map scale of 1:1000, points 1 cm apart on the map are 10 meters apart on the ground.

- 1:2000 1 cm on the map equals 20 meters on the ground
- 1:2500 1 cm on the map equals 25 meters on the ground
- 1:5000 1 cm on the map equals 50 meters on the ground
- 1:10,000 1 cm on the map equals 100 meters on the ground
- 1:15,000 1 cm on the map equals 150 meters on the ground

ACTIVITIES

These activities will help develop a sense of the relationship between distance on the map and the actual distance on the ground.

- Using any available maps with a clear scale practice measuring the distance on the map and use the scale to calculate the actual distance on the ground.
- The instructor marks out 100 m on a field with a marker at each end. Using double pace counting, i.e., counting each time the right or left foot hits the ground, participants carry out the following exercises:
    1 Count the number of double paces while walking the 100 meters and repeat until consistent.
    2 Count double paces while running easily, as in a cross-country point-to-point event.
    3 Where the terrain is suitable, individuals record their own double pace averages for running over the 100 m in the following types of terrain:

    Open, flat spaces

    Up hill country

    Broken ground areas

    Downhill country

There is still more knowledge that needs to be acquired on how to estimate distance, and this we will learn by "STEP-COUNTING".

This is a very old technique of judging how far away things are. The Roman soldiers used this technique and counted 'double steps' in groups of 1000. This was called the 'mille passus' in Latin and this is where the word mile came from and the actual distance.

To practice 'step-counting' we will need to be in an area of at least 100 meters. We will need a 100 meter tape, some markers, paper, and pencil.

Here is the practice

1   Walk the 100 meters and count every time the right foot comes to the ground. Write down the answer.
2   Walk back again, count, and write down the answer.
3   Repeat 1 and 2 again. Add these figures together and divide by 4 to obtain your personal step-count figure for walking 100 meters.
4   Repeat these same procedures, but this time run at a steady 'marathon' pace. The average figure you obtain this time will be your step-count figure for running 100 meters.
5   Try this same process but do it in rough terrain.

Points to note: Don't over-stride when walking and don't run 100 meters at a dash speed.

Exercise 1

Use the chart below to calculate your result

Number of DOUBLE STEPS in 100 m

	Open Space	Rough Area
Walking		
Try 1		
Try 2		
Try 3		
Try 4		
Average		
Running		
Try 1		
Try 2		
Try 3		
Try 4		
Average		

Number of DOUBLE STEPS for other distances

	Open space	Rough area
Walking		
50m		
200m		
400m		
1000m		
Average		
Running		
50m		
200m		
400m		
1000m		
Average		

It is important to note that traveling in the woods is very different from traveling in open travel areas and on the track. Take into consideration the obstacles that may slow you down or take you slightly off course in order to maneuver around.

All maps are reduced to a scale. In the case of these exercises the answers are based on a map that has a scale of 1:25,000. That means that the map has been reduced 25,000 times. Therefore, for every unit on the exercise map, there are 25,000 units on the ground covering the same distance. Because map scales are usually in 1,000's it is convenient to think metric when we want to estimate distance. An easy way to remember how to change different map scales into meters is to take away the last three zeros. The number left tells you the number of meters.

Hence on this exercise:

1mm = 25 meters on the ground
10mm = 250 meters on the ground
40mm = 1,000meters on the ground

Exercise 2

How far on the ground are these distances on a 1:25,000 scale map?

Distance	Answer in meters
1. 1mm	
2. 2mm	
3. 3mm	
4. 5mm	
5. 8mm	
6. 13mm	
7. 28mm	

Exercise 3

How far on the map (scale 1:25,000) are these distances on the ground?

Distance	Answer in mm
1. 50m	
2. 100m	
3. 125m	
4. 300m	
5. 550m	
6. 1,000m	
7. 1,250m	

Exercise 3

This exercise is based on a scale of 1:25,000. Measure the distance in millimeters and convert to meters for each distance. Make sure to measure from the beginning of one control to the beginning of another control or from the end of one control to the end of another control. Do not measure from the beginning of one control to the end of another control because this could add 5 mm which is equivalent to 125 meters.

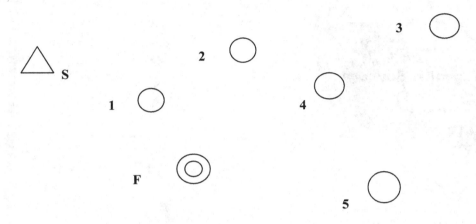

Direction	Millimeter	Meters
S to 1		
1 to 2		
2 to 3		
3 to 4		
4 to 5		
5 to 6		
6 to F		

Exercise 4

Carefully find all of the 'CONTROL POINTS' on the PRACTICE MAP. Read the control point descriptions to check that you have the correct place. Answer the questions in the table below by careful measuring.

How far is it between?		Answer in meters
A. Bridge	B. Field Corner	
C. Building	D. Ruin	
E. Power Line	F. Marsh	
G. Boulder	H. Cliff	
J. Pond	K. Summit	
L. Waterfall	M. Stream Junction	

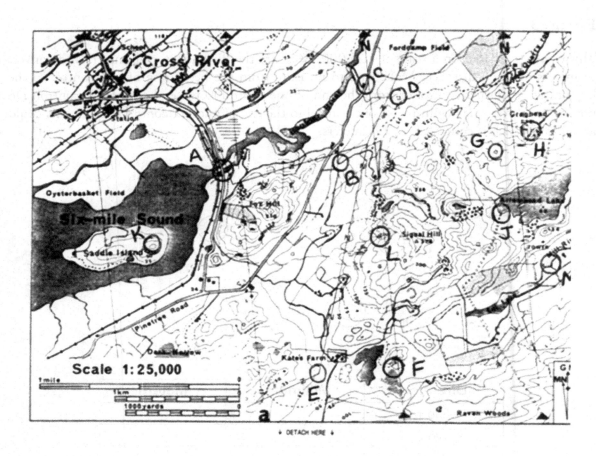

Scale 1:25,000

↓ DETACH HERE ↓

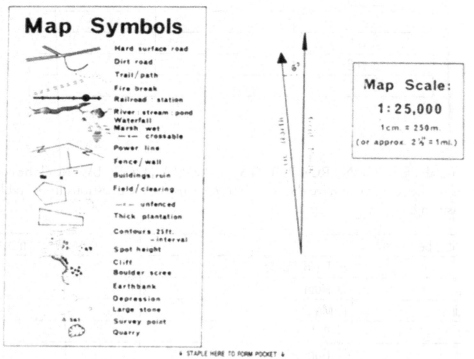

Map Symbols

Hard surface road
Dirt road
Trail/path
Fire break
Railroad : station
River : stream : pond
Waterfall
Marsh : wet
—··— crossable
Power line
Fence/wall
Buildings : ruin
Field/clearing
—·— unfenced
Thick plantation
Contours 25 ft.
— interval
Spot height
Cliff
Boulder scree
Earthbank
Depression
Large stone
Survey point
Quarry

Map Scale:
1:25,000
1 cm = 250 m.
(or approx. 2½" = 1 mi.)

↓ STAPLE HERE TO FORM POCKET ↓

Practice Map

ORIENTING THE COMPASS

1. **CARDINAL DIRECTIONS**
2. **COMPASS PARTS**
3. **ORIENTEERING BY COMPASS**

OBJECTIVE: To introduce directional terms and basic compass and map skills.

Review the four cardinal directions and relate them to the four cardinal points on the compass. Know the inter-cardinal directions as well.

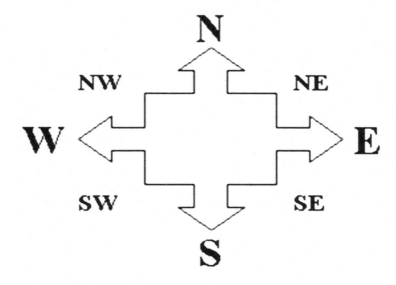

Try the compass direction exercise
in the supplementary materials to help teach directions.

CARRYING A COMPASS:

- Loop compass cord around wrist. Hold the compass in one hand.
- Place the compass level in the palm of your hand with the direction-of travel arrow pointing straight ahead, in line with the center of the body and about waist high.
- Keep the compass level or the needle may get stuck and not move properly.

EXERCISE ONE: FACING THE CARDINAL POINTS

Set the compass to each of the four cardinal points and in each case turn the body and the compass to face them. For example, line up the N on the compass housing with the direction-of-travel arrow. While holding the compass as explained, rotate your body until the magnetic needle is aligned with and points in the same direction as the orienting arrow. You will now be facing north. This is called putting RED FRED in the SHED.

EXERCISE TWO: DIAL-A-BEARING GAME

Call out a bearing (e.g. 115). Each student must orient their compass to that bearing and face it. Try a number of different bearings with the students. Remember you need to put RED FRED in the SHED and always follow the DIRECTION of TRAVEL ARROW.

EXERCISE THREE: LANDMARK BEARINGS

Face a landmark than aim the compass's DIRECTION of TRAVEL ARROW at the landmark and orient the compass. You will need to turn the compass housing until RED FRED is in the SHED.

EXERCISE FOUR: SCHOOL YARD COMPASS GAME
(STAR ORIENTEERING)

This activity is best set up on a baseball or softball field which will allow for natural boundaries.

Preparation before the activity: Set 8 compass bearings. Each bearing is to be taken from second base. Place a control marker with a letter or number at each of the bearings around the perimeter of the field. Make up control cards with bearings in mixed up order so that student's do not all go to the same location and have the same answers.

Objective: The students will be given a control card with 6 bearings in random order. All students are to take the bearing from second base. Once they set the compass to the proper bearing they are to follow the direction of travel arrow on the compass and walk out to the marker and write down the code letter or number that they find at that location next to the bearing.. They are to return to second base to take the next bearing and follow the same procedure they used for the first bearing. They are to follow this pattern until they have recovered all the code numbers or letters. When they are done they should check their results with the master card that the teacher made up based on where they set all the control cards.

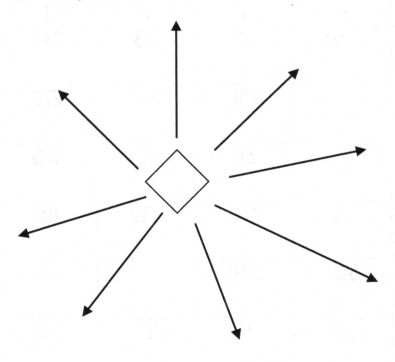

Sample game cards

a	b	c	d	e	f
10	10	180	340	340	50
50	150	230	270	85	150
340	85	150	85	270	340
230	180	50	230	180	180
150	230	10	10	150	85
270	340	340	180	50	270

g	h	j	k	l	m
230	150	270	85	340	150
10	10	230	270	270	50
340	180	50	340	150	180
150	85	150	230	85	85
50	340	340	180	50	270
270	230	10	10	180	340

TAKING A COMPASS BEARING FROM A MAP

- In order to read a map more easily, the map should always be oriented to the terrain.
- Orienteering maps have parallel lines, which run south to north over the map. These lines, known a Magnetic North Lines, help to establish the other three cardinal directions and act as a guide to determine north with a compass.
- Rotate the housing until the orienteering arrow points toward the direction-of-travel arrow.
- Place the compass level on the map aligning the base-plate edge with the magnetic north lines and hold the map and compass firmly together. Turn your body until the magnetic needle is aligned with the orienting arrow and points in the same direction as the magnetic north lines on the map. The map is now oriented and the compass may be taken off the map.
- Allow the magnetic needle to settle. Because the needle is fluid it must be given an opportunity to settle before it is read.

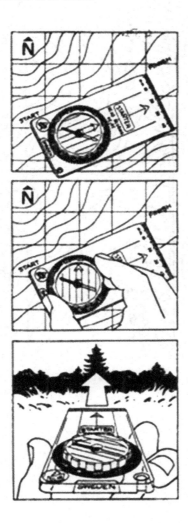

61

SETTING A MAP

The map is set when the symbols on the map are in direct relationship to the physical features on the ground. When setting a map with a compass, place the compass on the map. The map is then turned until the magnetic north lines are parallel to and pointing in the same direction as the red end of the magnetic needle.

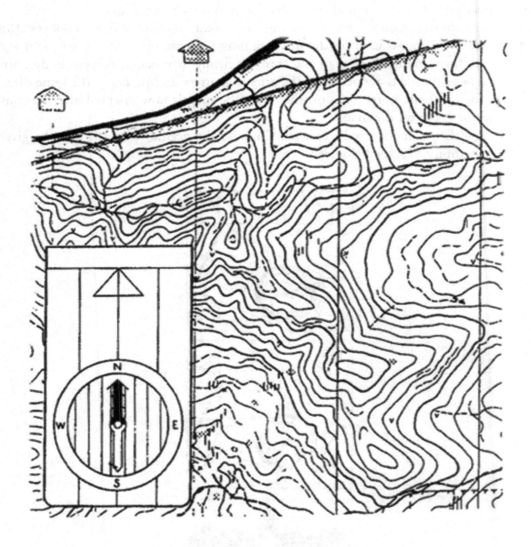

Take a bearing from a map.

In terrain with few features it is often necessary to use this technique. The following steps are taken:

Step 1: Place the compass on the map with the edge joining the two controls. The travel arrow must lie in the desired direction of travel.

Step 2: Turn the compass housing so that the orienting lines run parallel to the meridian lines on the map.

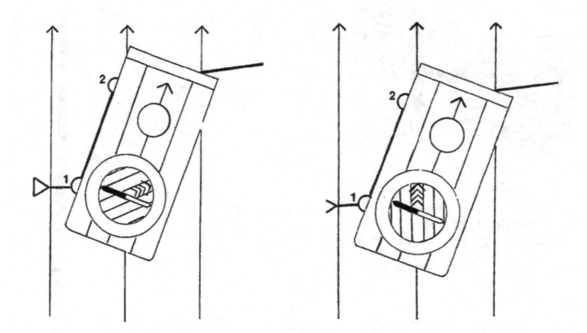

Step 3: Take the compass off the map and hold horizontal and square to the body at waist height. Turn your body until the red magnetic needle sits over the orienting arrow.

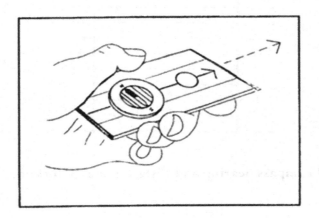

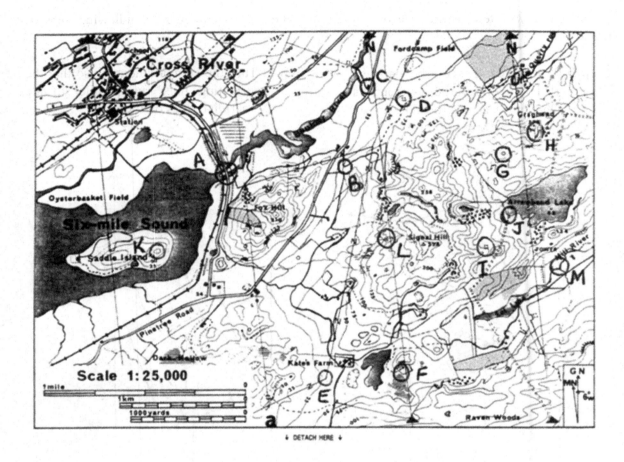

↓ DETACH HERE ↓

Directions			Degrees	Meters
A	⟹	B		
B	⟹	C		
C	⟹	D		
D	⟹	E		
E	⟹	F		
F	⟹	G		
G	⟹	H		
H	⟹	I		
I	⟹	J		
J	⟹	K		
K	⟹	L		
L	⟹	M		
M	⟹			
	⟹			
	⟹			

Practice map: Record compass bearing and distance to each location.

COMPASS ORIENTEERING

Even though orienteering is predominantly a game using maps and sometimes a compass it may become necessary to depend upon the compass and pacing to figure out where you are. In this activity no maps are used. Each student is given a control card with compass bearings and steps. It is important to set the exact bearings on the compass and pace out the distance as indicated. For this activity it is necessary to know the parts of the compass and how to carry and orient a compass. Key factors to consider:

- Always keep the compass level
- Do not try to read the compass around metal objects because this will affect the readings
- Make sure the direction of the travel arrow is pointing straight ahead, in line with the center of the body and waist high
- Turn your body not the compass while holding the compass level and steady until the magnetic needle is lined up in the red box
- Establish a pace by counting every second step (double space) between two markers.

Class Assessment: COMPASS COURSE & STEP COUNTING

Preparation before class: Make 2 sets of courses all with different bearings and steps. You can use the sample courses printed on the next page. One set of cards is to be given to each team to set the course and to write the code. The other set is to be given to the teams after all the courses are set. This set does not contain the code. Each team must try to figure out the code that the first team set.

Objective: Demonstrate compass skills by setting a course using step counting and setting a bearing.

Organization: Have the class get into teams of 5-6. Give each team a course code card with a starting number (1-8), a colored cone, and 5-6 poly dots of any number sequence. Each team will set up their course following the coordinates on their course card and counting out the 'double steps' for each bearing. Use the NUMBERED poly dots to make up a code for your team. Remind the students not to put them in numerical order but vary the sequence offering a greater challenge. Write the code next to the bearing and steps on the original course card and give it to the teacher. After all the courses are complete and the cards are collected, the teacher will give each team a new course card that another team set up and have them try to decipher the code by following the coordinates they set out. When the students are finished they should compare their results to the code card that the teacher collected from each team after they set their course. You may need to check students work for accuracy.

Sample Courses

	1				2				3	
Bearing	Steps	Number		Bearing	Steps	Number		Bearing	Steps	Number
85	7			180	5			10	4	
310	10			300	9			235	7	
230	5			80	6			130	8	
80	8			200	10			25	5	
310	10			265	8			200	10	
190	15			95	7			265	8	
	4				5				6	
Bearing	Steps	Number		Bearing	Steps	Number		Bearing	Steps	Number
150	6			270	5			230	4	
265	10			50	10			95	9	
95	7			120	6			20	6	
20	9			210	8			310	8	
310	6			60	6			235	4	
235	5			260	7			130	7	
	7				8					
Bearing	Steps	Number		Bearing	Steps	Number				
50	7			340	7					
290	6			120	6					
120	10			310	10					
240	4			190	8					
95	5			300	7					

MAP SKILLS

READING CONTOURS

It is important to know whether you will be climbing, descending, or on flat ground as you approach a control. One of the most difficult map reading problems is to visualize the landform patterns that contour lines represent and to relate the pattern of contour lines on the map to the terrain. Key features to look for:

- Contour lines FURTHER APART represent a gentler slope
- Contour lines CLOSER TOGETHER represent a steep slope
- Contour lines MERGING show a very steep slope and /or cliffs
- Contour lines CLOSED AROUND reflect hills or knolls
- Contour lines CLOSED AROUND with slope lines shown represent depressions.

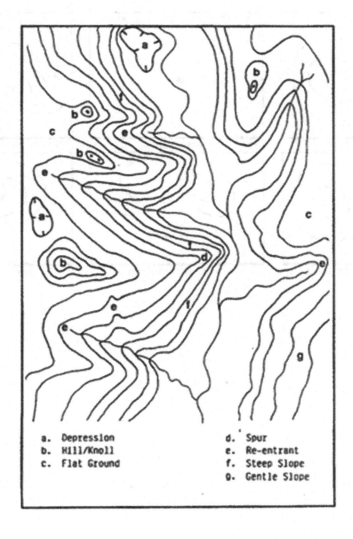

a. Depression
b. Hill/Knoll
c. Flat Ground
d. Spur
e. Re-entrant
f. Steep Slope
g. Gentle Slope

Landforms:

There are many different landforms, each with its own name. These are often used at control sites in orienteering and are identified by control descriptions.

- Re-entrant: A small gull or valley with no permanent watercourse
- Depression: A hollow with higher ground on all sides
- Knoll: A small hill
- Saddle: A low lying dip between two higher points
- Spur: A small ridge, usually steep and lying off a main ridge

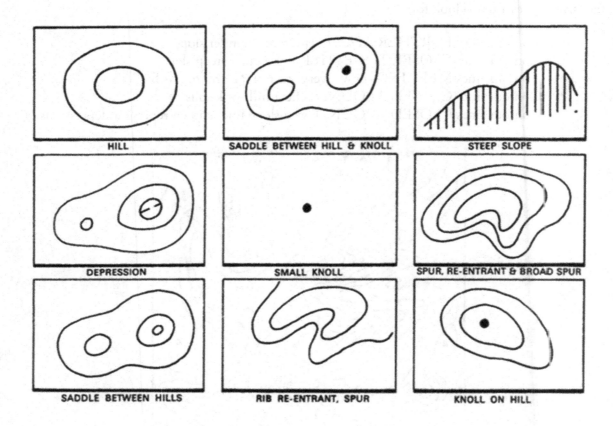

HILL   SADDLE BETWEEN HILL & KNOLL   STEEP SLOPE

DEPRESSION   SMALL KNOLL   SPUR, RE-ENTRANT & BROAD SPUR

SADDLE BETWEEN HILLS   RIB RE-ENTRANT, SPUR   KNOLL ON HILL

PUTTING IT ALL TOGETHER

Orienteering is all about choosing the best route and then using appropriate navigation techniques to travel between controls. While the shortest distance between controls is a straight line it is often not the easiest or fastest route. By following the route of least resistance the distance traveled may be greater but faster in terms of time.

ACTIVITIES

Path of least resistance

Evaluate each of the routes shown on the following map taking into account run ability and ease of navigation.

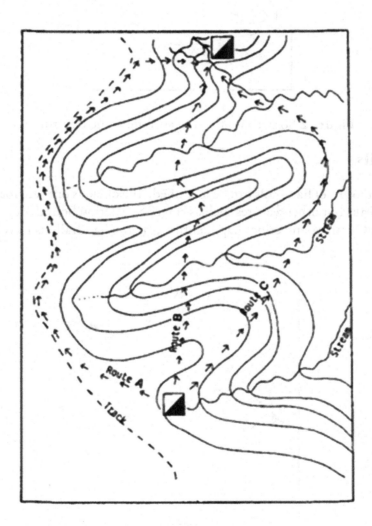

Figure 1 Route A follows a trail making this the best choice. The other two courses have nothing to follow to keep you on course.

Contouring

Hill climbing is very tiring and a route involving ups and downs will sap energy. It is better to work out alternative routes using contouring techniques to maintain height.

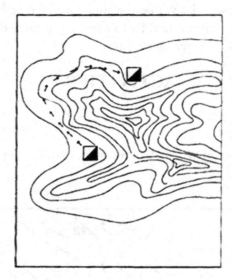

Figure 2 Sometimes the longer route is the best route.

Using handrails

Many different forms of handrails can be identified. The obvious ones are roads, tracks, fences, streams and firebreaks but other features such as ridges, vegetation boundaries and valleys can be extremely helpful. On an orienteering map identify as many handrails as possible.

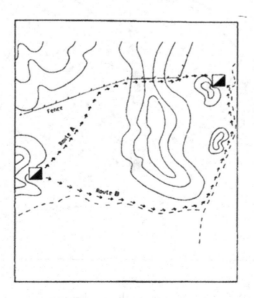

Figure 3 Route B follows a trail, Route A follows a fence.

Aiming Off

In situations where the line of travel will meet collecting feature, it is advisable to aim off to ensure you know which way to turn when you reach the collecting feature.

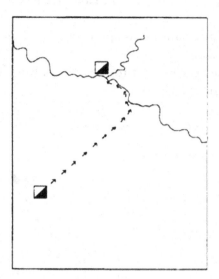

Figure 4 Purposely go too far right to meet the stream.

Attack Points

An attack point is a well-defined feature such as a trail junction, streambed, pond or hill. To be effective, the attack point should be reasonably close to the control. Once the attack point has been found, very carefully navigate to locate the control.

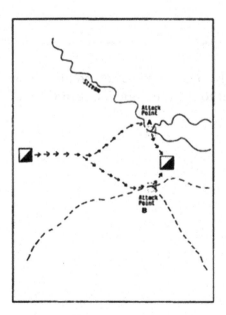

Figure 5 Attack Point A: Trail-Stream Crossing Attack Point B: Trail Junction

Traffic Lights

Travel from one control to the next can be likened to traffic lights.

- Green: Once a route choice has been made progress is fast to the nearest handrail or collecting feature
- Orange: As the end of a handrail is approached and an attack point has been selected extra care must be taken
- Red: Travel from the attack point to the control must be done very carefully using a compass bearing or fine navigation.

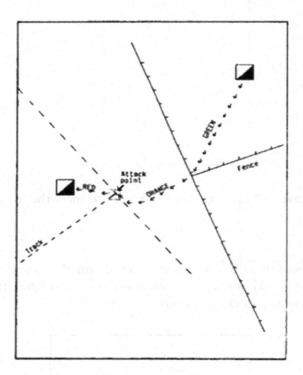

Figure 6 Move quickly to get to fence corner. Slow down as you try to find the trail. When you get to the trail junction scan the area for the control site.

Relocation

When unsure of your position the temptation is to search for the control. However, it is important to relocate by finding a recognizable feature, which can be used as an attack point. Often it is necessary to retrace your steps to a collecting feature that was passed.

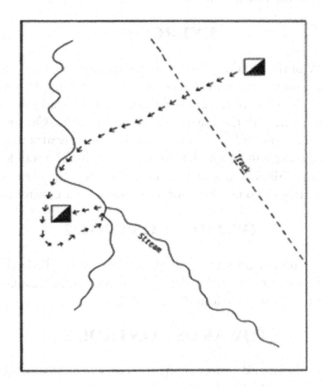

Figure 7 Follow the stream to the stream junction in order to navigate to the control site.

A MAP WALK

Use the PRACTICE MAP to help you go through the map walk. Read through the text below and carefully follow the line on the map.

EXERCISE:

Start at a trail to the NW of the building. Travel south passing under a power line until you come to a main road. Turn east on the main road. The first thing you should pass will be a boulder on the left side of the road. Use close observation skills to find the trail that comes up on the right side of the road. Follow the trail all the way to the first control site. On the way mentally tick off land features that you pass. You will first come to cabins. Shortly after the cabins you will have to do some climbing and there will be a rock field on your right. The trail levels off and continues all the way to a stone wall. This is your attack point as the first control site is located by the stone wall. You have found control site one. Don't forget to mark your control card.

TOWARDS CONTROL 2

After leaving Control 1, you get on a trail going west. There is a little climbing to do but not much. You pass a marsh on your left and a cliff face on your right. Just beyond a second marsh you come to a trail junction. You have found Control 2.

TOWARDS CONTROL 3

Follow the trail to the northeast and almost at one you come to another trail junction. The control site is located at the base of a cliff. You have found Control 3.

TOWARDS CONTROL 4

To find control site 4 you will need to use your compass to set the bearing to follow. You will need to go around the marsh. Look for some object across the marsh that you can use as a landmark. Once you get across the marsh check your compass bearing and follow the compass until you come to a spur. There a many small rocks to the north of the spur. You have found control site 4.

TOWARDS THE FINISH

We continue traveling south until you meet a trail. Take the trail to the north until you come to a group of cabins. We have finished our map walk.

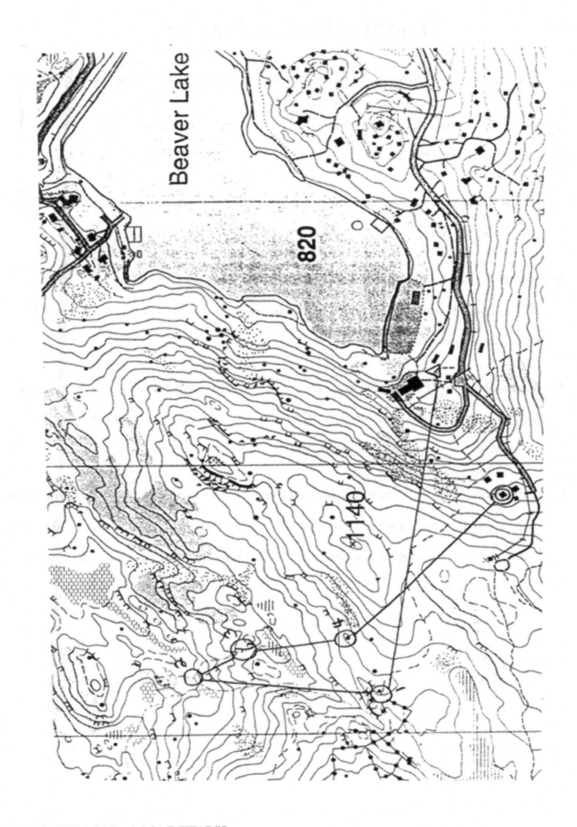

PRACTICE MAP: A MAP WALK

Helpful Hints to Navigate

1. Keep the map set (orientated) at all times and move the thumb along the line of travel.

2. Check the control description carefully. Is it at a trail junction by a boulder? Know what you are looking for.

3. Check the terrain surrounding the control and select an attack point. Look to see if the control is by a fence corner, a trail-stream crossing, a stone wall, etc.

4. Identify useful handrails and collecting features. Can you follow a trail or a stream? What types of things did you pass along the way? Were there cabins, an entrance to a cave, a large boulder?

5. Mentally check off features as they are observed. If the map says that you are to turn right at the third trail junction beyond the marsh make sure you count off the trail junctions as you pass them so you do not turn too early or too late.

6. Identify and note any catching feature beyond the control in case you overshoot. If the map says that there is a stone wall after the attack point and you come to the stone wall before you find the control site this will let you know that you have gone too far and need to go back.

CHOICE OF ROUTE

During an orienteering race or on a competitive hike, the decision on which route you take from one control to the next is yours alone. You will want to find a quick and economical way, but it also needs to be safe. The route you chose should not leave you too much guess-work in the final stages.

With the help of the map you must try and establish which way is best. You should remember that good trails usually follow valleys and streams, and that a good navigator utilizes 'handrails' as he goes through the terrain, like the edge of a field, power lines or walls, as well as the more obvious guide lines.

In the situation below, you are at control 1 and all set to find control 2. You set the map and study the alternatives. Think, than make your choice. Which is the best route A, B, or C?

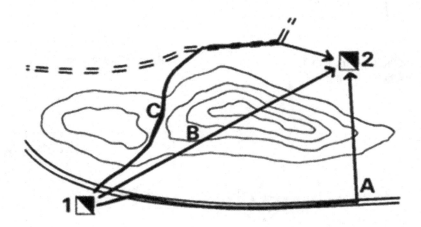

Commentary on the 3 Routes:

A. Fast but very unsafe. It will be difficult to know exactly where to leave the highway. No attack point.
B. Very unsafe and tiring. This is a tough climb over the hill. It is hard to stay on a compass course for such a long session.
C. Obviously the best choice. This course is quick and safe. The bend in the dirt road will make a fine attack point for the last few meters into control 2.

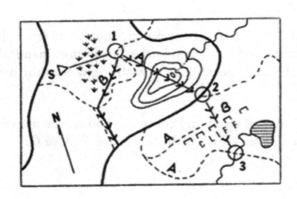

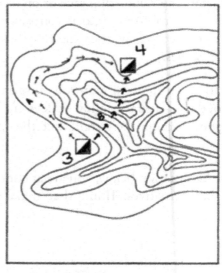

Route Choice from 1 to 2
Route Choice from 2 to 3

Route Choice from 3 to 4

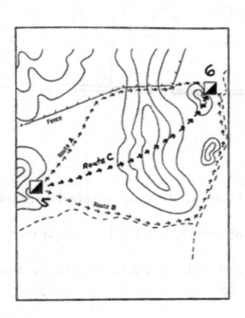

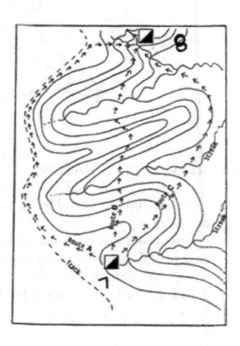

Route Choice from 5 to 6

Route Choice from 7 to 8

ROUTE CHOICE EXERCISE

In this exercise you will try to make the best route choice and explain why that is the best way to go. Take into consideration:

- Climb versus Detour
- Short hard route versus Long easy route
- Handrails and Collecting features

1. From 1 to 2 the best route is _____.
Explain:_____
_____

2. From 2 to 3 the best route is _____.
Explain:_____
_____

3. From 3 to 4 the best route is _____.
Explain:_____
_____

4. From 5 to 6 the best route is _____.
Explain:_____
_____

5. From 7 to 8 the best route is _____.
Explain:_____
_____

SKILL DEVELOPMENT
SETTING THE COURSE

Course lengths should range from one to 2.5 kilometers with 8-12 controls. Remember much of the fun in orienteering is finding the markers.

- Orient the map by terrain in order to read it, and establish the four cardinal directions (N, S, E, and W.)
- Choose a route by using handrails (roads, paths, fences, edges of fields, etc.) in order to establish a safe, reliable, and fast route between controls.
- Use collecting features, (intersecting roads or trails or natural features) which will give you an opportunity to check and see if this is where you think you are.
- Be aware of the basic compass parts. The orienteering compass is used three basic ways:
    1. To orient a map.
    2. To measure distance on the map.
    3. To establish a direction (bearing) from the map to guide you in following that bearing.
- Establish the actual distance between control points and/or key map features. This will involve learning and understanding the metric system, and changing millimeters to meters, etc.
- Establish a pace by counting every second step (double space) between two markers. Try walking and running distances of 50 meters and repeat it several times to establish a pace.
- Try different variables in pace counting such as going up a hill, down a hill through the brush, etc.
- Be able to use contour lines to see the difference between hills and valleys and whether or not you are dealing with steep or flat terrain. Contour lines close together reflect steepness and when far apart, flatness.
- Orient the compass. Set the compass to each of the 4 cardinal points and in each case turn the body and the compass to face them. Also take a compass bearing on a landmark. Face a landmark, aim the compass's direction-of-travel arrow at the landmark and orient the compass.
- Test different types of terrain to establish its traverse-ability in terms of:
    1. Climb vs. detour
    2. Short hard route vs. long easy route
- Practice selecting attack points. The presence of a large, distinct, and reliable attack point is often the deciding factor in making your route choice. Find the large attack points first, such as the corner of a field, a path junction, or the bend in a stream, and then with precision compass and pace counting, move onto the smaller feature.

NAVIGATION TECHNIQUES

QUESTIONS TO ASK BEFORE MOVING

1   What is the feature at the control site? **Check control description and feature in the center of the circle.**

2   What lead me to the control? **Handrail(s)**

3   How will I know I am almost there? **Attack point**

4   How will I know I have gone too far? **Collecting feature**

5   What major features will I see along the route to the control? **Check off features**

6   Fold map to show where you are and just beyond where you are going.

7   Orient map using land features and compass, if necessary.

8   Place thumb on map where you are and move as you reach other major features along your route.

At the control site

1.   Compare control description code with code on the control flag. **Punch only if they match.**

Repeat the process for each of the controls.

LESSON NINE
THEME: CROSS-COUNTRY ORIENTEERING

OBJECTIVE: To challenge map reading abilities in an activity suited for a large area that is partially wooded.

MATERIALS

- Master map with clearly defined boundaries
- Set of blank maps and control cards and control descriptions.
- 8-12 controls hidden within the wooded area.

PREPARATION

1. The course should range in length from 1-2.5km with 8-12 controls. The distance to the first control should be a little longer than the rest in order to spread participants out at the beginning.

2. Avoid placing controls, which force participants to double-back.

3. The controls must be placed sequentially and they must be found in the order indicated on the map.

ACTIVITY

This is the "traditional" Orienteering used for most competitions.

1. All controls must be found in the order indicated on the map.
2. Have everyone place their name on their control card and attach a map with the control points and control descriptions to it.
3. Begin at the start triangle indicated on their map.
4. Each member should carry the maps with them and "follow" or "thumb" their way from one control to the next.
5. Make sure to match the control site with their control description before marking the control code on their control card. Make sure the proper numbered box is marked on the control card.
6. When the course is completed hand in the control card so that it can be scored for accuracy.
7. This activity can be done in pairs or individually and may be started with a staggered start of 30-second intervals, or as a mass start.

This activity is a great way to finish up the unit on Orienteering. Plan a trip to a site that offers orienteering. Many maps are available on the orienteering web site that may be purchased or down loaded.

Cross-country Orienteering is the standard competitive form of orienteering and requires a little more organization and more time than the previous lessons. Try to discourage teams from following one another or putting controls in repeating or backtracking patterns. This will prevent participants going to control 4 seeing people leaving 4 to go to 5. In other words, control 4 requires little or no orienteering skill to locate. The way to prevent this from happening is by adding a control. Remember the fun is in the discovery.

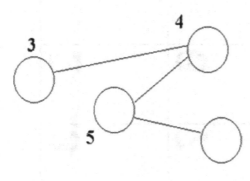
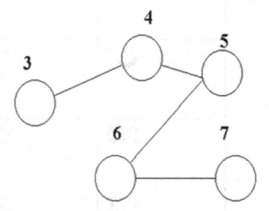

4	8	5	1
3	7	6	2
2	6	7	3
1	5	8	4
4	8	5	1
3	7	6	2
2	6	7	3
1	5	8	4

Start Time _____   Number
Finish Time_____

Total Minutes_____

List Team Members Below:

1) _____
2) _____
3) _____
4) _____
5) _____
6) _____

Start Time _____   Number
Finish Time_____

Total Minutes_____

List Team Members Below:

1) _____
2) _____
3) _____
4) _____
5) _____
6) _____

Start Time _____   Number
Finish Time _____

Total Minutes_____

List Team Members Below:

1) _____
2) _____
3) _____
4) _____
5) _____
6) _____

Start Time _____   Number
Finish Time _____

Total Minutes_____

List Team Members Below:

1) _____
2) _____
3) _____
4) _____
5) _____
6) _____

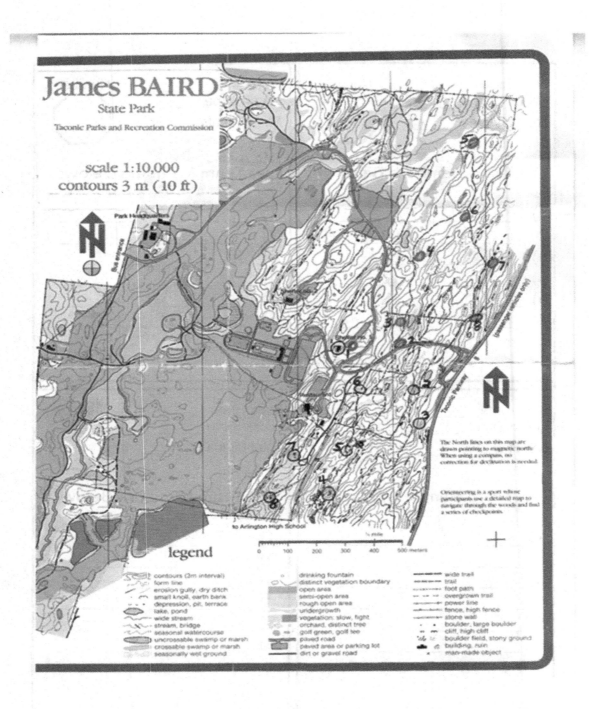

Figure 2 Two courses are set. A red and a yellow course each with a common starting area and 7 control points.

MAKING A SCHOOLYARD MAP

In order to draw a simple sketch map of a schoolyard you will need to do some planning and a little field -work. Careful preparation and attention to detail will take time but is necessary to make a map that is accurate and one that can be used over and over.

Follow these steps to prepare a sketch map of a schoolyard.

Step 1: Equipment
You will need the following equipment:

- Pencil
- Graph paper
- Compass
- Data chart

Step 2: Determine the scale of your map.

a) Decide the size of the area to be mapped.
b) Do this by pacing off the area. Figure out how many paces you take in 10 meters and figure out from there. It doesn't have to work out exactly.
c) If you use standard paper 8 ½ X 11, a suitable scale for an area 150m X 200m would be 1cm to 10m, which should allow the map area to fit on the paper.

Step 3: Determine what will be included in your map.

Decide what features (buildings, trees, basketball courts, etc.) you want and choose a symbol to represent each. A typical map legend should appear at the bottom to the map and may look as follows:

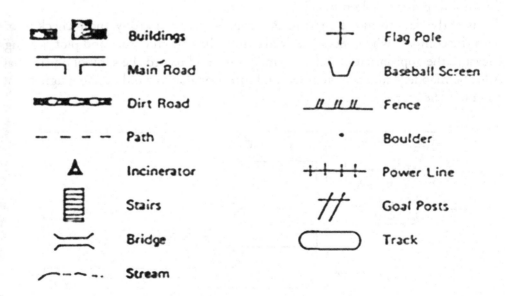

Buildings	Flag Pole
Main Road	Baseball Screen
Dirt Road	Fence
Path	Boulder
Incinerator	Power Line
Stairs	Goal Posts
Bridge	Track
Stream	

Step 4: Draw Magnetic North.

Draw parallel lines 4cm apart across the paper from the top to bottom and write NORTH at the top.

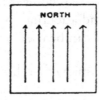

Step 5: Gather Data.

    a.   Begin at one corner of the area to be covered by your map. (The corner of the school is a good reliable feature around which to sketch the rest of the map).

    b.   From your chosen corner take the bearings on the objects you wish to include in your map. Pace the distance to each object. Record bearing and distance on the data sheet. (See Data Sheet Supplement)

    c.   Calculate the map distance using the distances on the data sheet and the scale you selected.

Step 6: Drawing the Map

    a.   It is important to have features located accurately relative to one another.

    b.   Begin in the corner of your map that corresponds to the corner from which you took your bearings (building).

    c.   Transfer the bearings to the map and measure the proper distance from the corner and draw the proper symbol.

    d.   Transfer bearings to map, set compass for bearings given on data sheet. Lay compass on map with base plate touching corner or reference point. Turn entire compass until orienting arrow is lined up with magnetic north line. (Compass base plate should still be against corner and bearing should remain unchanged. Measure the appropriate map distance to put symbol on map.)

    e.   Transfer the data from the chart to the map. Measure carefully and recheck bearings with the compass when necessary. Walk from the chosen corner and plot bearings. Measure the appropriate distance in map units and record the symbol on the map.

    f.   Add the map legend, scale, symbols and directional arrow indicating magnetic north to complete the map.

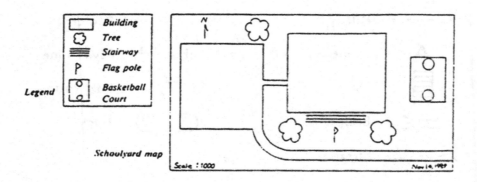

88

DATA SHEET

OBJECT	SYMBOL	BEARING	DISTANCE PACES	MAP DISTANCE

Sample sketch map

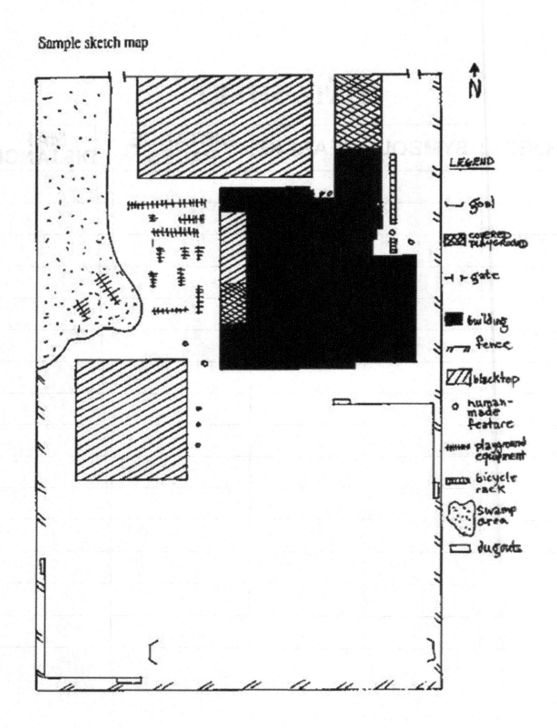

LEGEND

⌐ goal

▨ covered playground

⊢⊢ gate

■ building

ᴨᴨ fence

▨ blacktop

○ human-made feature

⊢⊢⊢ playground equipment

▭▭ bicycle rack

⬭ swamp area

▭ dugouts

ORGANIZING & RUNNING A SIMPLE ORIENTEERING MEET

EQUIPMENT

You will need the following:

- A MAP
- CONTROL MARKERS
- PENS, PENCILS, OR PUNCHES
- CONTROL CARDS
- WHISTLE
- WATCH
- COMPASSES

THE MAP

Any map that helps you meet your objectives for the event will do. However, there must be a map. It can be:

- A floor plan of a building, if you are holding the event inside.
- A sketch map of your schoolyard or property.
- A street map with the names of the streets removed.
- A map of a local park.
- A USGS topographic map.

NOTE: Make sure that you have permission to use the area in which you will run your event.

THE CONTROL MARKERS

You need some way of identifying each control site for the participants. A regulation Orienteering marker is an orange and white triangular sleeve made out of nylon or vinyl board. However, you can use your imagination and make markers out of almost anything. Just make sure they are recognizable and not too small.

GLOSSARY

- **Orienting the map** Arranging or holding a map so that the symbols on the map are in the same position as the features they represent on the ground. The map can be oriented either by comparing the map directly with the terrain (orienting by terrain) or by using the compass (orienting by needle).
- **Scale** the relationship between distances on the map to distance on the ground. This information is expressed as a ratio (1:25,000) or as a bar graph on the map.
- **Control** the man-made or natural feature in the landscape upon which a marker is placed, and which is described by a clue.
- **Control marker** Usually a red and white, or orange and white, three dimensional nylon marker used to mark the control location, and equipped with a paper punch and a letter code for orienteering use.
- **Control circles** A circle drawn around a feature on a map to indicate the site at which a control marker is located. The center of the circle is the exact location of the control marker in the terrain.
- **Master map** A map on which the control circles of an orienteering event are drawn and from which each orienteer marks her own map at the start.
- **Folding and thumbing** Fold your map so it shows only the part you need to see at the moment. Use your thumb as a pointer to direct your eye to where you are on the map. This helps you keep on course better and to always know where you are on the map.
- **Handrails** Linear features in the landscape, which help to guide you along a route choice. Examples include trails, roads, streams, fences, stone walls, re-entrants, ridges, contour lines, and vegetation boundaries.
- **Collecting features** those natural and man-made features, which we pass en-route to a destination and tell us that we are on course.
- **Catching features** A large feature, usually linear, beyond a destination, which will "catch" or alert us if the destination is passed. May be used as an attack point.
- **Attack Point** A large feature near a destination which can be used to determine one's exact position and from which careful and precise navigation to the destination can be made.
- **Plans of attack** A Plan or organized approach to finding the control, or the attack point.
- **Route choice** the route one selects to follow on the map and in the terrain to a destination.
- **Safety bearing** A compass bearing or direction which will lead directly to a road or a major trail, and which an orienteer can follow to obtain help if lost or injured, or in the event of an emergency.

REFERENCES

Garrett, Mary E. Orienteering and Map Games for Teachers, U.S. Orienteering Federation, 1996.

Gilchrist, Jim, Orienteering—Instructors Manual. Canada: Orienteering. Ontario Publication, 1984.

Hicks, Ed. Orienteering Unlimited, Inc.

Silva Orienteering Services, USA.Teaching Orienteering, Binghamton, NY, 1991.

Wilson, Peter. Orienteering: A Way of Learning Outdoor Navigation, Hillary Commission, 1997.

Materials

Supplement

CONTROL CARD

CONTROL NUMBER	LETTER
1	
2	
3	
4	
5	
6	
7	
8	
9	
10	
11	
12	
13	
14	
15	
16	

MYSTERY "O"

Name: _____ Class Period: _____

SUSPECTS	found
Ms. Tisdale	
Mrs. Snow	
Dr. Pipps	
Mr. Brown	
Mr. Parker	
WEAPONS	
Revolver	
Tire Wrench	
Rope	
Dumb Bell	
Knife	
ROOMS	
Auditorium	
Garage	
Hall	
Lounge	
Study	
Kitchen	
Dining Room	
Court Yard	
Elevator	
Laboratory	
Library	

Color Codes			
Green	Red	Orange	Purple
Yellow	Blue	Black	Black

TRIVIA ORIENTEERING GAME CARD

#	TRIVIA QUESTION	ANSWER
1		
2		
3		
4		
5		
6		
7		
8		
9		
10		
11		

SCORE ORIENTEERING GAME CARD

Time Limit: 15 minutes
Penalty: 5 pts per minute late

Control #	Control Letter	Control Value	Control Description
1.			
2.			
3.			
4.			
5.			
6.			
7.			
8.			
9.			
10.			
11.			
12.			
13.			
14.			
15.			
16.			
17.			
18.			
19.			
20.			

Total Points	
Penalty Points	
Final Score	

VEGETATION BOUNDARY	**PERMANENT BENCH**
PERMANENT TABLE	**UNCROSSABLE MARSH**
POND	**CLIFF FACE**
CONIFEROUS TREE	**DECIDUOUS TREE**
TREE STUMP	**DRY DITCH**
TRAIL/STREAM CROSSING	**FENCE CORNER**

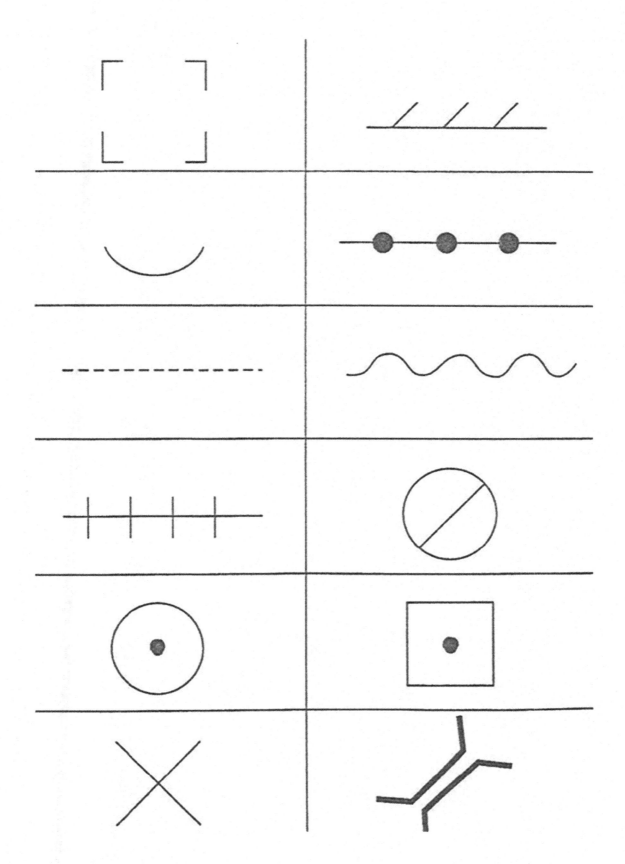

RUIN	FENCE
DEPRESSION	WALL
TRAIL	STREAM
POWERLINE	SEWER
SIGN POST	FLAGPOLE
ROOTSTOCK	BRIDGE

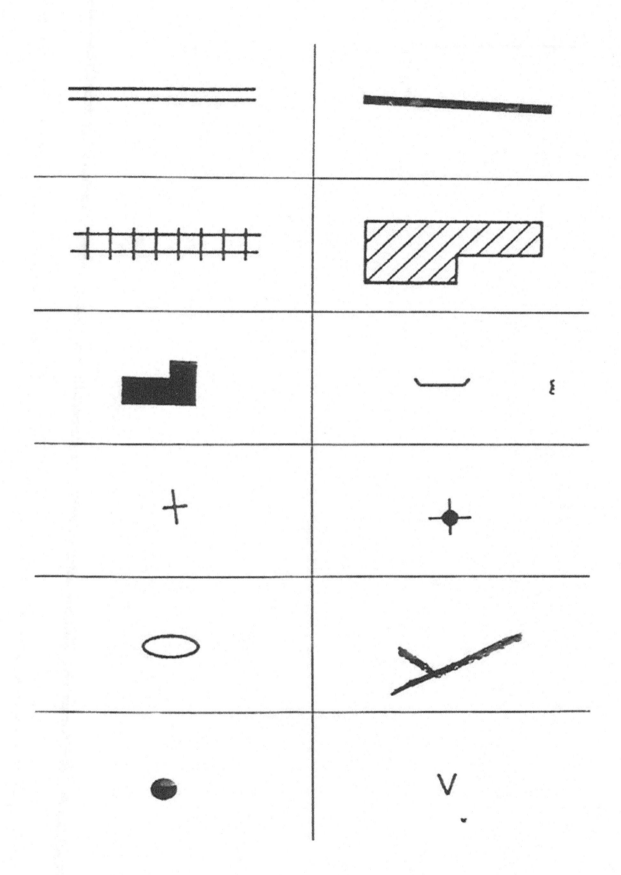

MAIN ROAD	**DIRT ROAD**
RAILWAY	**PARKING LOT**
BUILDING	**GOAL POST**
PLAYGROUND EQUIPMENT	**LIGHTPOST**
SMALL HILL (KNOLL)	**TRAIL JUNCTION**
BOULDER	**PIT**

PRACTICE MAP

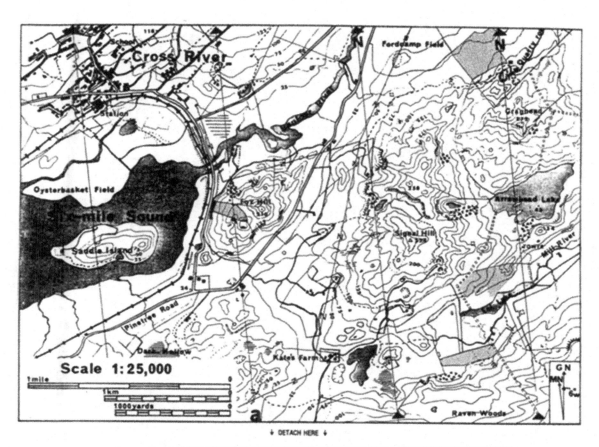

↓ DETACH HERE ↓

Directions		Degrees	Meters
A → B			
B → C			
C → D			
D → E			
E → F			
F → G			
G → H			
H → I			
I → J			
J → K			
K → L			
L → M			
M →			
→			
→			

Scale: 1:25,000 1mm = 25m Read bearings to the nearest degree

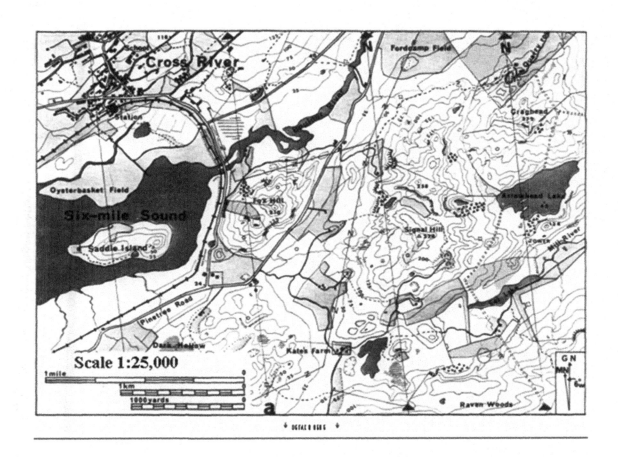

Practice Map

Compass Direction Exercise

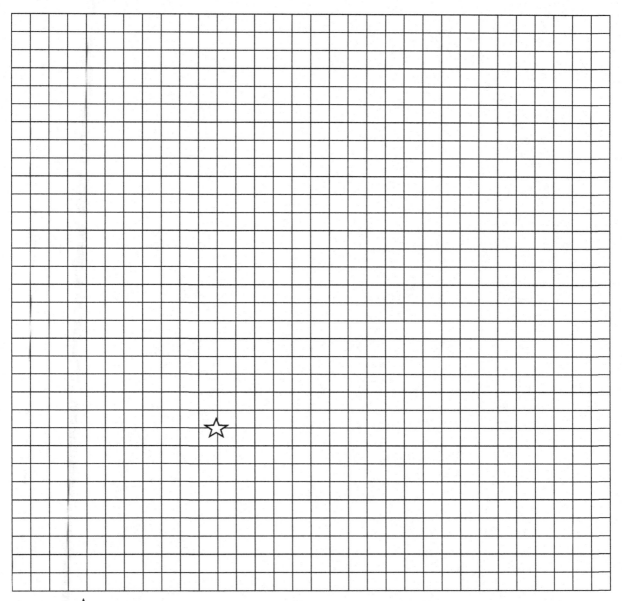

Start at ☆
1 square = 100 Meters

1. 100 N	8. 200 E	15. 200 W	22. 400 S
2. 200 W	9. 300 N	16. 100 S	23. 400 NW
3. 200 NE	10. 200 NE	17. 200 E	24. 400 SW
4. 200 E	11. 200 SE	18. 200 SE	25. 400 N
5. 100 N	12. 300 S	19. 200 W	26. 200 W
6. 200 W	13. 200 E	20. 100 S	
7. 200 NE	14. 200 SE	21. 200 W	

TRIVIA ORIENTEERING GAME CARDS

What is the capital of New York?	**What two primary colors make purple?**	**What is another name for the first day of spring?**
Name a state that starts and end in the same letter.	**Name an exercise that will improve abdominal strength.**	**How many laps around the track equal one mile?**
List the four Cardinal directions.	**List the four Inter-cardinal directions.**	**What two primary colors make green?**
What is another name for the first day of winter?	**In 2012 the summer Olympics was held in this country?**	**List one health related fitness component.**
What river runs through the grand canyon?	**In the game of soccer there are how many players on the field for each team?**	**When you hit a home run with bases loaded this is called?**

SCORE ORIENTEERING GAME CARD

A 5	B 5
C 10	D 10
E 15	F 15
G 20	H 20

I 5	**J** 5
K 15	**L** 15
M 20	**N** 20
P 10	**R** 15

S 20	T 20
U 10	V 5
W 15	X 20
Y 10	Z 20

PART TWO

GPS Technology
In
The Classroom

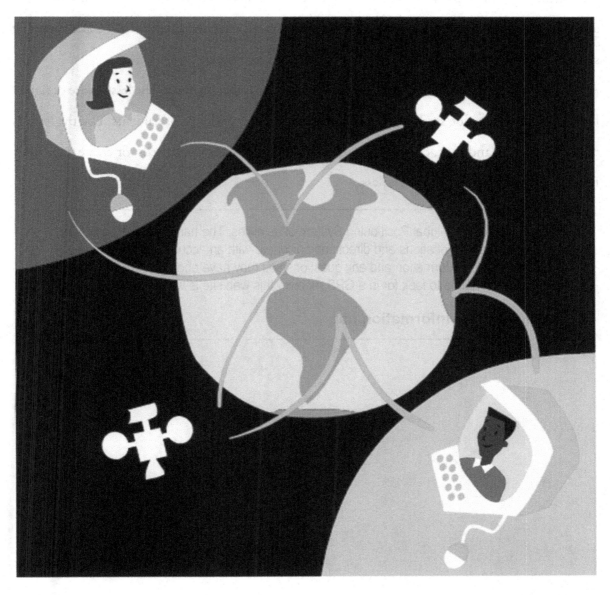

By Nancy Kelly

Why GPS in the Classroom?

GPS technology can be used as an educational tool in enhancing student understanding of scientific inquiry, language arts, physical education, geography, math concepts, problem solving, as well as personal development.

The students will develop vital communication skills and analytical thinking to complete hands-on, inquiry based, collaborative projects that require higher order thinking skills. The worksheets that accompany every lesson require the students to know how to ask critical question and communicate affectivity in order to solve problems. The students will use GPS and mapping skills to provide problem based learning and authentic assessment.

All lessons and activities align with the National Standards in education. The lessons are designed for use with 4th-8th grade students, but can be used for all age groups of students. Use the lessons provided in this handbook, change them to meet your own classroom needs, or create your own. Remember, the possibilities are endless.

GPS stands for the Global Positioning System of satellites. The handheld GPS receiver can be used to find locations and directions anywhere with an accuracy of up to 6 feet. For more detailed information and any questions you may have about the GPS system as well as what features to look for in a GPS receiver this web site is very helpful.

http://www.gpsinformation.net

Part Two GPS Technology Table of Contents

Geo-caching for the Classroom

Objective: Learn how to locate a position. Ask the question "Where Am I" and learn about the use of the compass, the difference between Relative and Absolute locations, and how to use latitude and longitude lines to determine locations.

<u>Pre Lesson Discussion</u> - Relative Position

"Where Am I"- Lead a class discussion and have the students describe where they are in location to another student, to the cafeteria, to another town, to the ocean, to another country, to the sun, moon, and stars. We need to be able to document and understand our location in order to find our way. What tools and methods can we use to "find our way"? We can use anything from landmarks and directions (turn right at the stop sign) to compasses and maps.

Activity: This game teaches about relative position and keeping mental notes. Position the students around you. Explain to the students that they are all at a relative location on the planet based on where they are standing in relation to you. They are also at a relative position to everyone else in the room. Some students are to the right of you, across from you, behind you and next to you. As you move around the relative positions will change. This is where the fun begins. Their movement is based on relative positioning. Tell everyone to go to a partner who is opposite them, N goes to S, E goes to W. etc. This is their Flip Flop Partner. Next tell them to go to someone next to them. This is their High 5 Low 5 Partner. Now move to someone far away from them. This is their Round the World Partner. Next go to the person closest to them. This is their Wringer Partner. For the last exchange, go to someone opposite them, N goes to S, E goes to W. This is their Missed High 5 Partner. Every time the students move to new partners their relative position keeps changing. Have them go back to each of their partners performing the skill they learned with that partner. Now try to mix it up randomly calling out different partners they are to go to. Tell everyone to keep their feet moving at all times and move to the correct partner as you call out the directions. How did they do? Were they able to find all their partners and do the proper movement with them? Do they understand how their relative position to objects and people in the room keep changing based on their movements?

Directions:

Flip Flop: face partner and do patty cakes (one hand up one down and keep switching after you hit your partner's hands)

High 5 Low 5: face partner and give a high 5 right than left hand and follow with touching feet together right than left.

Round the World: face partner and join hands above your head and holding hands move them out and down to your thighs and clap hands.

Wringer: face partner and hold hands twist as you go under each other's arms. Go in both directions.

Missed high 5: face partner and do a missed high 5 and follow by leaning down and grabbing their leg and hop.

Lesson 1 Using a Compass

Hold the compass in one hand. Place the compass level in the palm of your hand with the direction of travel arrow pointing straight ahead, in line with the center of the body and about waist high. Keep the compass level or the needle may get stuck and not move properly.

Exercise 1 Facing the Cardinal Points

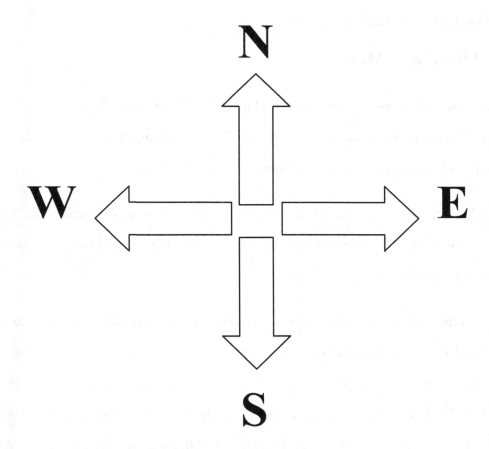

Set the compass to each of the four cardinal points and in each case turn the body and the compass to face them. For example, line up the N on the compass housing with the direction of travel arrow. While holding the compass as explained, rotate your body until the magnetic needle is aligned with and points in the same direction as the orienteering arrow. You will now be facing north.

Go outside and try this simple exercise.

1. Record your specific location. Example: Under the stone arch in the back of the school and the date.

2. Set the compass to N and face that direction.

3. List things exactly to your North. List only permanent objects and try to be as specific as possible.

4. Do the exercise facing E, S, and W.

Exercise 2 Reading a Map

Find a street map and use specific landmarks and directions (N, S, E, & W) to take a scenic tour of the town. How many points of interest did you visit? Could you direct someone else to visit the same points of interest by using good landmarks and directions?

Find a Tour Map of a historical area like the Freedom Trail in Boston, Massachusetts. Take the freedom walk and circle the points of interest along the trail. Write down how you would direct a tour group through the site.

Activity: One important skill for following directions is having good recall or memorization skills. Put out 15 unrelated items. Give the students 1 minute to memorize as many of the items as they can. Go to a different location give everyone a piece of paper and see how many items they can remember. Did they know how many items there were? This is vital when going on an expedition. You need to know how many sites to visit before you take off. How did everyone do? Could they at least recall 10 items? Did anyone remember all 15 and know that there were 15 items?

Lesson 2 Compass Angles

There are 360 degrees on a compass: 0=N., 90=E., 180=S., and 270=W. Compass directions are absolute in terms of location on maps and the globe but compass directions are relative to your location.

Mark off a large circular area. Line the students up E to W facing north. Have them all take a reading on their compass to a designated spot (flag pole). Have the first person on the line (furthest E) be exactly at O degrees (N) to the object. Record all the findings in the boxes.

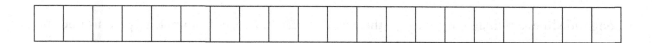

Why were all the readings slightly different?

You can also illustrate this on a globe. The directions you call north depend on your location. Locate New York and locate Lake Ontario. What direction do you need to travel to get from one location to the next? If you started in Montreal would you have to travel in the same direction? Therefore N., S., E., & W. are relative directions. One student near the front of the classroom will have different people to the N., S., E., & W. of them compared to another student near the back of the classroom.

Pre Lesson Discussion: Absolute Directions

Absolute directions are needed in order to get to an exact location therefore it is necessary to have a known point of reference or a fixed reference. Latitude and longitude lines provide a fixed reference point.

Latitude lines are imaginary lines on the earth's surface. They run east to west around the globe and tell you your distance north or south of the Equator. Think of latitude as the rungs of a ladder. The rungs lie east to west but they tell you how high you can move up or down.

Longitude lines are imaginary lines on the earth's surface that run from pole to pole around the globe and tell you your distance east or west from the Prime Meridian. Think of long telephone poles (longitude lines run from pole to pole).

Latitude and longitude lines are measured in degrees. Since the earth is a circle, and in mathematics all circles are measured in degrees, it was decided to measure latitude and longitude in degrees also. The first latitude line is the equator (equally distant from the north and south poles). Thus the equator is recorded as 0 degrees and all other latitude line are measured in degrees north or south of the equator. There are a maximum of 90 degrees of latitude north of the equator and 90 degrees of latitude south of the equator. The first longitude line is the Prime Meridian. Thus the Prime Meridian is recorded as 0 degrees of longitude and all other longitude lines are measured in degrees east or west of the Prime Meridian. There are a maximum of 180 degrees of longitude to the east or the west of the Prime Meridian.

Factoid: Why was the Prime Meridian selected as the first longitudinal line? The prime meridian was selected by international agreement at the International Meridian Conference called by President Chester Arthur in October of 1884. Representatives from 25 nations met in Washington and made the decision.

Activity: Play a game of quick line up. Have the students form a box around you so you have students N, S, E, and W of you. Tell the students that you are the intersection of the equator and prime meridian and everyone around you is at an absolute location somewhere on the planet. As you rotate or revolve they must always go to their absolute location.

Move to a new spot and have the student's line up facing you in the exact position they were first in when you started the activity. If they were north of you and the third person from the right they should be still north of you and the third person on the line from the right no matter where you moved to and what direction you are facing. Keep moving around and see how quickly they can adjust to the new location and still stay in the same absolute position to you all the time.

Lesson 1 Absolute Directions

In order to answer the question "Where Am I?" you need to be precise and use clarity when communicating positions to someone else. Directions need to be given based on an agreed upon reference or some coordinate system.

Activity One: Place two students back to back and give them each a checker board. See if they can duplicate placement of the checkers by giving accurate descriptions of where to place the checkers. Have the students describe to each other where to place the checker, so that each checker is in the same position on each board. How did they do?

Activity Two: Try the same activity but this time instead of moving checkers move each other and see if they can duplicate their movements. The students should begin by standing back to back with their partner and see if they can accurately describe their movements so their partner will be able to mirror this movement. Remember to mirror a movement, if moving left they must tell their partner to move right. If moving forward in a right diagonal they must tell their partner to move backward in a left diagonal. How did the students communicate their locations?

Using Latitude and Longitude

When trying to locate someplace on a map we may use street names. Latitude and longitude lines are like imaginary street names on the earth. When using latitude and longitude lines to give directions it is customary to give the latitude first and the longitude second. To find a latitude line such as 66 degrees north latitude, you must do three things:

1. Go to your starting line (the equator).
2. Determine which direction you must go (north or south).
3. Determine the distance in degrees you must go (66).

To find a longitude line such as 35 degrees east longitude, you must do three things:

1. Go to your starting line (the Prime Meridian).
2. Determine which direction you must go (east or west).
3. Determine the distance in degrees you must go (35).

If you find the intersection of these two imaginary streets, you have found the exact (absolute) location of a particular place on the earth's surface.

Activity One: Play a game of cops and robbers. Using a local street map try to move robbers from the bank they just robbed to the get-away car without the cops capturing them. Make sure you avoid any streets that cops are patrolling on. Driver in car must relay accurate information.

Set up: Teachers will need to place cut out patrol cards on the map at random locations.

*Alternative: Find a picture of a maze and see if the students can communicate how to get through the maze to another student.

Activity Two: Divide the class into two equal teams. Place 2 sets of numbered poly dots on the ground representing lines of latitude and longitude. The coordinate (0, 0) represents the intersection of the equator and the prime meridian. Call out a coordinate and one person from each team needs to move to the poly dot that represents that coordinate. They should both land on the same poly dot number. Challenge team A against team B to see which team lands on the most correct numbers. Use as many coordinates as members of the team.

Sample: (5, 2) (2, 3) (3, 5) (1, 4) (6, 3) (4, 5) Key (11, 14, 27, 19, 18, 28)

How did they do? Can they locate a position based on lines of latitude and longitude?

1. Interactive games using poly dots

A	31	32	33	34	35	36
	25	26	27	28	29	30
	19	20	21	22	23	24
	13	14	15	16	17	18
	7	8	9	10	11	12
	1	2	3	4	5	6
0,0						

B	31	32	33	34	35	36
	25	26	27	28	29	30
	19	20	21	22	23	24
	13	14	15	16	17	18
	7	8	9	10	11	12
	1	2	3	4	5	6
0,0						

Describing a Location

In order to introduce absolute reference frames for describing locations, students will learn to provide accurate directions using Cartesian coordinates (x, y axes in geometry and algebra) and latitude and longitude on the globe.

Activity One: Label a piece of graph paper or a drawn grid as shown on the practice sheet. Have the students find positions communicated as follows (1, 2), where the first number represents movement to the right from zero along the horizontal axis and the second number describes the distance to move up along the vertical axis. You can have the coordinates mark out a simple design like the exercise below or you can use the coordinates to sink battleships, etc.

7									
6									
5									
4									
3									
2									
1									
0	1	2	3	4	5	6	7	8	9

Have the students draw a simple picture from the following lines between the given sets of positions.

(4, 1) to (4, 4) (4, 1) to (5, 2) (5, 2) to (5, 5)

(1, 4) to (1, 1) (1, 1) to (4, 1) (1, 4) to (4, 4)

(1, 4) to (2, 5) (2, 5) to (5, 5) (4, 4) to (5, 5)

Discus what information is needed to communicate points and drawings. For example, each line required information about a starting point and an end point.

Experiment # 1

Objective: Use latitude and longitude to find locations on a map.

Materials needed:

1. White paper
2. Large box graph paper with blue vertical lines and red horizontal lines
3. Pictures of animals

Procedures:

1. Have the students pretend that they are working at a zoo and they have to make up a map that tells us where the animals are located.

2. First give the students a piece of white paper and have them place the animals anywhere they would like on the paper. Now have them explain to someone else the exact location of the animals on the paper. Students should find it difficult to pinpoint the exact location.

3. Ask the students what would make it easier for them to locate the animals on the paper. Lead the students to conclude that lines on the paper would help them locate the animals.

4. Discuss vocabulary terms: parallel, longitude, latitude, equator, prime meridian.

5. Have the students place these works in there note book.

6. Discuss the use of latitude and longitude lines. Explain how these help people find their way to exact locations. Give the students the piece of graph paper with the blue and red lines.

7. Have them locate the center red line and mark it with a 0. This will be the equator. Have them number the lines above the center line from 10 to 90 (10 point intervals) and to do the same below the center line. These are the lines of latitude.

8. Have them locate the center blue line and mark it with a 0. This will be the prime meridian. Have them number the lines to the right (east) and left (west) of the 0 from 10 to 90 (10 point intervals). These are the lines of longitude.

9. Now have the students place the animals on the graph paper. Have them mark down the exact location of the animals by recording the latitude and longitude coordinate.

Take a globe and have the students find a location based on the latitude and longitude coordinates. Next have the students find a location on the map and have them identify the coordinates. Have the students identify various cities, historical landmarks, geographic features using latitude and longitude.

Additional Assignment

Take a trip to 5 countries of your choice via the internet in the "take a brief trip" screen.

- Find a country. Click on it. Describe the surrounding area.

- Put in latitude and longitude coordinates.

- Tell what you see in the picture. Try to pick out as many interesting features as you can find.

- Do this for 5 countries of your choice.

- Place an X on a map at the point where the picture was taken.

Have the students try to match the proper latitude and longitude coordinates to the major league football teams. Can you find the coordinates to the major league baseball teams?

*Go to these lessons on Latitude and longitude for more ideas for the classroom

http://academic.brooklyn.cuny.edu/geology/leveson/core/linksa/latlong_menu.html
http://geographyworldonline.com/tutorial/

Fun Activity: Key Pad

Objective: Decipher coordinates by using the numbers on a phone pad to locate volcanoes (or historic landmarks).

Equipment:

- Floor tape to make a phone key pad (substitute with numbered poly dots)
- A topographic map of the world with volcanoes.
- Colored markers

Activity:

1. Divide the students into groups of 3-4. One student is the coordinate master. They hold the seUcret coordinates that the other 3 students must try to decipher. Once the coordinates are found one of the team members must go to the world map and locate the volcano.
2. Place an X with the colored marker next to the volcano.
3. Go back to the key pad and try to figure out the coordinates for the next volcano.
4. Continue in this fashion until all the volcanoes have been located.

Procedure: The teacher gives one of the members of the team the latitude and longitude coordinates for 5 volcanoes. They are not to give this information to anyone else on their team. The first coordinate is for latitude. The # is for N and the * is for S. the first team member steps on the # or the * to find out whether the first coordinate is N or S. If they are correct the operator says BEEP and they can move on to try to find the first number. If they are correct again the operator will say BEEP and they can go on to find the next number. If they are wrong the operator will say BUZZ and the next person on the team must repeat the sequence from the beginning and then move on to find the next correct number. If they get buzzed the 3rd person on the team will repeat the sequence trying to find the next correct number. To find the longitude coordinates again start with the # or the *. The # represents E and the * represents W. Keep going until all the coordinates have been found and then try to locate the volcano on the map. Remember to have everyone on the team start at the beginning as they are trying to locate all the coordinates. For example if the coordinates are N36 E139, the last person to find the final coordinate needs to step on all 7 parts of the sequence. The first team to locate all the volcanoes correctly is the winning team.

Sample coordinates

N36	E139
N60	W030
S27	W109
S90	E010
S90	W180

7	8	9
4	5	6
1	2	3
*	0	#

Lesson One: Degree Confluence Project

Objective:

1. Identify the intersections of latitude and longitude on Earth.

2. Visit one or more of the integer degree intersections of latitude and longitude.

3. Post photographs of each visit on line or for a classroom scrap book.

4. Write a narrative of the posting.

Factoid: The total number of degree confluences is 64,442, (179 lines of latitude, multiplied by 360* of longitude plus, the 2 poles + 179 x 360 + 2 = 64,442), of which 21,543 are on land and 38,409 are on water. There are 16,324 primary degree confluence points. A confluence is primary only if it is on land or within sight of land.

Procedure:

1. Give the students a map of the world or a map of one of the continents. The map should have lines of latitude and longitude.

2. Give each student a posting of several of the indexed primary degree confluence points and see if they can locate them on their map.

3. Tell the students to select one of the sites that they located and to write a narrative of the posting.

4. Have the students draw a picture of what they may expect to find at the location they chose.

This lesson is multidisciplinary and can be used to identify such things as landforms, climate conditions, industry, agriculture, culture, art appreciation, etc.

Additional Assignment:

Have the students find a primary degree confluence point close to where they live and to take a photograph and write a narrative and to post it online. If they are going on vacation over one of the holidays have them try to find a primary degree confluence point at their vacation site and take a picture of it and write a narrative and post it online.

Lesson 2 Locating Points of Interest

Have the students explore their neighborhood for interesting items. They can be anything such as: dunkin' donut shops, ball fields, odd color houses, funny mailboxes, farm tractors, etc. They are to post its location and take a photograph of the items so that others can find it too.

Lesson 3

Use the above lesson but this time look for interesting objects or places anywhere in the world. The students can be doing a lesson on South Africa and look for locations in Johannesburg. They may follow the expeditions of Marco Pole and try to locate places he travelled to. Other ideas may be National Parks in the United States, the Seven Wonders of the World, the journeys of Lewis and Clark, etc.

> Visit www.confluence.org online to check out the degree confluence project. The goal of the project is to have people visit every area on the Earth where latitude and longitude lines intersect and to take a picture and document your journey there.

Satellites

A satellite is any object that orbits or revolves around another object. The moon is a satellite for the earth and the earth is a satellite for the sun. Man-made satellites give information on weather, scientific research, navigation and more. This unit will focus on the navigational uses of satellites primarily the GPS. GPS, which stands for Global Positioning System, is the only system that can give you exact locations anywhere around the world. There are more than two dozen GPS satellites circling the earth twice a day in a very precise orbit and transmit signal information to the earth. These signals are monitored by ground stations located worldwide. Anyone with a GPS receiver can detect these signals. The GPS receiver compares the time a signal was transmitted by a satellite with the time it was received. The time difference tells the GPS receiver how far away the satellite is. The GPS will take readings simultaneously from 3-4 separate satellites and with distance measurements from all the satellites, the receiver can determine the user's exact position.

There are 2 parts of all satellites, the "payload" and the "bus". The payload is everything that the satellite needs to do its job, like a camera, antenna, radio, and electronics. Each satellite carries a different payload depending upon its job. The bus is the part of the satellite that carries the payload or all the equipment and helps to transport it around the earth and communicate with the earth.

Activity One:

Have the students find a partner. The pair represents one satellite, one is the "payload" and the other is the "bus". Have each student come up with a unique sound (animal sounds, traffic noises, clapping hands, stomping feet). Have everyone scatter around the room and close their eyes. As the "satellites" move around with their hands up in a bumper position to avoid collisions they repeat their "unique" signal. The traveler stops when they hear the signal they were listening for and they have found their missing half of the satellite. (The BING satellite is attached).

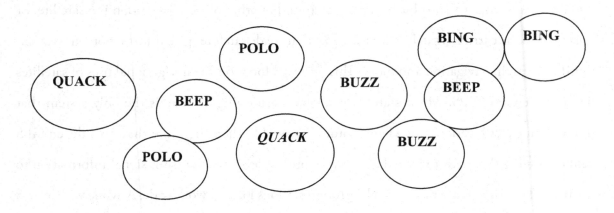

Satellites help travelers calculate their latitude, longitude, altitude, speed and direction of travel with accuracy to within 30 feet. Over 2 dozen satellites orbit at 11,000 nautical miles (about 12,500 miles) above the earth and transmit signals to ground stations worldwide. GPS receivers take this information and use triangulation to calculate the user's exact location.

Triangulating from satellites

A GPS triangulates from 3-4 satellites out of over 2 dozen available satellites in the system, so a traveler can find out where he/she is anywhere on or above the earth.

STEP 1: Knowing that we are 11,000 miles from a particular satellite narrows down all possible locations we could be on the globe to within a radius of 11,000 miles.

STEP 2: Next we measure a distance to a second satellite and find that it is 12,000 miles away. So we are somewhere on a sphere 11,000 miles from satellite 1 and 12,000 miles from satellite 2. Therefore, we are somewhere on the circle where these 2 spheres intersect.

STEP 3: If we make a measurement from a third satellite and find that is 13,000 miles away that narrows our position down even further to the 2 points where they all intersect. Only one of these points is actually on the globe the other point is usually miles away from the earth. Thus we have found our location.

Activity One: Find the Lost Hiker

1. Explain that the class has to locate one of their classmates who went out on an orienteering expedition and got lost. The lost hiker is trying to relay information back to the class so that they can come and rescue him. Have one student volunteer to be the lost hiker.

2. Ask for a second volunteer to be the lake that the hiker can see a short distance away. Place the volunteer about 8 feet from the hiker and give them a hoop to hold.

3. Ask a group of students to be the rescue squad. They need to ask the hiker questions about his location so that they can get a better idea where he may be. The questions may be if the hiker knows whether they are N., S., E., or W. of the lake and how big the lake is.

4. Add a second landmark (another volunteer) to be the water tower that is higher up on the mountain from where the hiker is standing. Place the volunteer about 6 feet away

from the hiker holding another hoop so that the lost hiker, the lake and the water tower form a triangle.

5. The lost hiker now has two points of reference for the rescue squad when asked to describe his location. "I have a lake to my right and a water tower to my left "

6. Add a third point of reference: a large boulder 6 feet away from the hiker. Ask for a fourth volunteer to be the boulder and have them hold another hoop. Now there are 3 points of reference, the lake, the water tower and the boulder which form a triangle around the lost hiker.

7. Now have the rescue squad ask the lost hiker for his probable location. "I can see a lake to my right, a water tower to my left, and a giant boulder behind me.

Have the 3 volunteers with the hoops move closer together so that the hoops all meet at one location (where the lost hiker is). Using 3 points, the team can now triangulate the position of the lost hiker.

8. Explain to the students that this is how GPS works. Instead of lakes, water towers, and giant boulders, and other landmarks, it uses highly-accurate satellites as points of reference. Instead of relying on vision to estimate one's location and distance, handheld receivers communicate constantly with the orbiting satellites, triangulating on at least three of them. This enables the receiver to display one's position to within 10 meters. You can add more landmarks and thus more hoops. Intersect all the hoops. The more satellites involved the more accurate the location.

Activity Two: Suppose that the Cartesian coordinates are mapping a portion of the ocean and that the distance of each square is the distance it takes a radio signal to travel one millisecond. There are three ships at sea, the Alexandria is at (0, 0), the Dorian is at (1, 5), and the Barrymore is at (6, 3). Each ship receives a distress signal from a fourth ship, the Houdini. The time that it takes the distress signal to travel to the 3 ships will help the ships locate the Houdini's position. On a piece of grid paper, go to position (0, 0), and draw a radius of 4 units with a compass. With position (1, 5) as the center, draw an arc with a radius of 2 units that intersects with the first arc. Finally draw a third arc, with a radius of 3.5 units with a center at (6, 3). Find where they intersect. Can you find the Houdini?

Signal travel time

SHIP	LOCATION	MILLISECONDS
Alexandria	(0, 0)	4.0
Dorian	(1, 5)	2.0
Barrymore	(6, 3)	3.5
Houdini		

How the GPS unit works

Activity 1

Objective: To calculate the relative accuracy of the GPS unit

Procedure: Choose a location on the school grounds. You are to take (5) readings at that site and average the readings.

1. Turn the unit on and allow it to acquire its position.
2. Write down the coordinates and elevation in the area shown below.
3. Repeat the process every minute until you have five (5) sets of data. Use your inboard clock on your GPS unit to tell time.
4. Calculate the average of the latitude, longitude and the elevation.

	LATITUDE		LONGITUDE		ELEVATION	
	ddd.dddd	N/S	ddd.dddd	E/W		
1.						
2.						
3.						
4.						
5.						
Average						

Activity 2

Objective: to search for a specific navigational waypoint

Procedure: five (5) sites have been selected on campus, coded ALPHA, BETA, GAMMA, DELTA, and EPSILON.

Locate the coordinates for your site in the WAYPOINT list of your GPS unit.

Using the GOTO function, locate the site on campus. Write the message that is found on the marker at the site.

"	"

Activity 3

Objective: to follow a track from one waypoint to another.

Procedure: ten (10) sites have been selected on campus, all coded with three letters.

You will be assigned a series of (5) numbers from the set (1, 2, 3, 4, 5, 6, 7, 8, 9, 10).

What is the number of your series? _____

Write the numbers for this series in these boxes

Following the order of the numbers and using the GOTO function, locate the sites on campus.

Write your sequence of codes here.

Activity 4

Objective: Students will be able to determine the latitude/longitude of an object and record the position.

Procedure:

1. Instruct students on how to acquire satellites.
   a) Go outside to a relatively clear area

b) Turn on the GPS receiver

c) Hold receiver so antenna is horizontal and visible to the sky

d) Wait until receiver gives indication that a position has been acquired.

2. Assign groups some object (examples- tree, bench, flagpole, score board).

3. Record the latitude/longitude that is displayed on the receiver for that object.

4. Have the students compare their positions and discuss error/accuracy of position.

5. Record the position again and compare if it changed from the first.

Worksheet

Object to determine position _____

Initial position:

    Latitude: _____N

    Longitude: _____W

Is your position similar to other groups' position?

Why the difference in position?

Record the object again.

Ending position:

    Latitude: _____N

    Longitude: _____W

Is there a difference between the first and second position?

Activity 5

Objectives:

- Explore the operations of the GPS Unit
- Recognize use of latitude and longitude coordinates in navigation
- Use GPS unit to orient your direction of motion and position

Instructions:

1. Look over GPS receiver; view each of the different displays. Find the screen to:

*Display Coordinate Position.

2. Go outside and find a clear area, turn on receiver and wait until satellites are located and position is calculated.

3. Find a feature and record its latitude and longitude. (Point A)

_____   _____   _____

      Feature   latitude   longitude

4. Measure out and try to walk 200 ft. due west and record new position. (Point B).

_____   _____

      Latitude   Longitude

How can you tell that you were going due west?

5. Walk for approximately 200 ft. due north and record new position. (Point C)

_____   _____

      Latitude   Longitude

How did you use the receiver to direct you due east?

6. Calculate how much the latitude actually changed when you walked north?

Latitude of Point B: _____

Latitude of Point C: _____

Difference in positions: _____

7. If one degree of latitude is approximately 70 miles, calculate the distance between the two positions.

8. If one degree of latitude can be divided into 60 minutes and one minute can be divided into 60 seconds, calculate the time difference between the two positions.

9. Calculate how much the longitude actually changed when you walked west?

Longitude of Point A: _____

Longitude of Point B: _____

Difference of positions: _____

*Fun activities that the class can do on the internet.

http://www.pbs.org/wgbh/nova/longitude/gps.html

Geo-caching

Imagine thousands of people working alone or in groups, moving about the globe undetected using a high tech treasure hunting device (GPS) to track down secretly hidden objects. This high tech treasure hunting game played by people all over the world with the use of a GPS device is known as "Geo-caching". The basic idea is to find hidden treasures or containers, referred to as 'geo-caches' and then share their experience with other people anywhere in the world.

A cache can be as small as a film canister and as big as a box. They can be artfully hidden in the wilderness, in places like hollow trees or under rocks, or they can be hidden in plain view yet they go completely unnoticed by people walking by. Each cache may contain a little treasure, like a key chain, but the real game is not the prize rather the hunt. Some caches are easy to find and in some cases you may need to climb, swim or row a boat.

www.geocaching.com: The original web site of the adventure game "geocaching". The web site is filled with helpful tips, terminology, links, and forums. Find out which geocaches are hidden near you! http://www.geocaching.com/seek/You can even hide your own 'cache' and log your container on the web site allowing anyone in the world to locate and log their find online.

Exercise One:

Objective: Develop skills of observation

Procedure:

1. Go into a room and have the students explore the room for 5 minutes and tell them to try to remember as much information as they can.

2. Leave the room and have them answer as many questions accurately about the room as possible.

   - How many windows were in the room? Doors?

   - What was sitting on the right front corner of the teacher's desk?

   - Did the room have a clock? A pencil sharpener?

   - On what window was the flower pot?

   - What word was written on the chalk board?

3. Return to the room and see how well you did.

Exercise Two:

Activity: Have the students go around the classroom looking for 15 hidden treasures (in this case letters). They can be concealed in objects like the tissue box or they can be in plain view like the American flag but detected only by careful observation.

Set Up: Hide 15 letters around the room. Have the students search for the letters by using careful observation and without drawing suspicion to alert the other students of their find. Tell the students they are looking for 15 letters hidden around the room and the 15 letters when unscrambled spell out a secret message, in this case 'TREASURE HUNTING".

Lesson One: Grand Slam

Objectives:

1. Use the GPS to calculate distance.

2. Collect, organize, display, and interpret data for a specific purpose or need.

3. Compare group results by determining the mean, median, and range, and explain what each indicates about the data.

Materials:

- GPS receivers for each group

- Large open field

- Kickball's

- Object to mark start and finishing points

- Field sheets

Procedure:

1. You will not need to mark waypoints ahead of time.

2. Take the students out to a ball field or any large open area where they have plenty of room to kick a ball.

3. The students will divide into groups of 4-5 and go to some spot on the field and find the waypoint for home plate. (You can review this procedure of imputing waypoints with them in their groups before they start the activity).

4. The student with the GPS receiver will stand out in the outfield. Their job is to track the final position of the kicked ball without interfering with it in any way.

5. Once the ball stops the outfielder is to input a waypoint for the ball at its location.

6. Have every member of the group kick the ball and input all the waypoints into the GPS unit.

7. The students can have 3 tries but only record the farthest waypoint into the GPS unit.

Back in the classroom:

Once the students get back into the classroom have them do the following:

1. Draw a rough map of their playing field and record on their maps the locations of each kick for their group. (Use different colored markers for each of the students)

2. Using the receiver find the distance between home plate and each kicked ball and mark that distance on their maps by drawing a line from home plate to the kicked ball and labeling its length.

3. Take the field sheets and use the information to calculate mean (add up all the distances and divide by the number of kickers) also calculate the median, range and the distance from the shortest kick to the longest kick.

4. You may want to compare all the class results into one big chart thus establishing a group mean, median, and range.

Lesson Two: The Amazon River

Level: Intermediate

Objectives:

1. To search for navigational waypoints

2. Use teamwork and problem solving to complete a task

Materials:

- GPS receiver

- Map of the school fields

- 20 poly dots

- 16 magic stepping stones

- 2 16-20ft ropes

- 2 scooters

- 4 Xerox pictures of wooden platforms

Getting Ready:

This Geo-caching event needs to take place in 2 stages. Stage One will involving finding the 5 waypoints and collecting the props to solve a problem. Stage Two will involve the students working together to problem solve and complete the challenge.

Stage One

Procedure:

1. 10 sites have been selected on the school grounds; 5 in option A and 5 in option B. (Try to hide them as best as possible so they cannot be seen from a distance away)

2. The coordinates for the 5 waypoints in each option will be marked on a 3 by 5 index card.

3. Divide the class into 2 teams and have them randomly choose one of the two cards (A or B).

4. Each waypoint will have one of the following props:
   - 10 poly dots
   - 8 magic stepping stones
   - 1 rope
   - 1 scooter
   - 2 Xerox pictures of wooden platforms

5. Try to visit all 5 waypoints in order to have all the props for the initiative.

6. The students should record its location and waypoints on the map.

This is the end of the first part of the challenge. They may only use the material they have located for the second part of the challenge. (Instead of the actual props you may just have index cards that explain the props they can use).

Stage Two

SURVIVAL: Amazon River

Your team is stranded on a Volcanic Island which is destined to erupt at any time. Your task is to get everyone off the island and back to the main land where everyone will be safe.

TASK: Using the props provided get everyone to the main land.

- The Islands (mats or platforms) can be used during the transport but they cannot be altered in any way or moved.
- The poly dots may be placed in the water as permanent rafts that cannot be moved once they have been put in place.
- The foam pads (Magic stepping stones) can float magically in the water but they lose their magical powers if they are left in the water by themselves. Therefore, someone must be in contact with them at all times or else they will drift away and become useless. You may not slide the magic stepping stones in the water nor use them in any other way but to step on them.
- The scooters are jet skis that can be used anywhere but only one person can ride them at a time. Arms and legs must never touch the water.
- The rope can be used any way the team wishes for support. The rope does not float.
- No one can touch the water because it has been contaminated with a deadly Ebola virus that eats away at your body.

GOOD LUCK

Back in the classroom it is now time for the students to research the Amazon River which is the largest river in the world. The students will meet in their cooperative groups and look up information about the Amazon River. The teacher can assign specific topics for the students to investigate.

Lesson Three: Team Relay Geo-Caching

Objective:

1. Students will organize a relay event

2. Use strategies to accomplish a task in the least amount of time

3. Calculate average time over a 2 day event

Materials:

- Florescent tape (use different colors for each team)
- Map of school ground

Procedures:

Make this a three-day event. The first day the students will form into three teams. Each team will be assigned an area of the fields around the school that they will set up their geo-caching course on. They are to have 5 cache sites (you may need to set up more or less depending upon the number of people on a team) that should be clearly defined on their maps giving the exact location and the waypoint Make sure that they only mark clear boundaries (corner of fence, edge of building, goal post, bleachers, sign posts, etc.).

Day Two the teams will go out and put the control markers at the cache sites. Use the rip-away florescent caution tape that you can find at any hardware store and secure it at each location. It is a good idea to number each of the strips that are put out so they know that they picked up the right cache marker. Give each team about 10 minutes to complete this task.

After this is done have the teams exchange control cards that have the location of the hidden caches on them with one of the other teams. On the signal (whistle) one team member from each team will go out to try to locate one of the caches. When they do they should run back give the control card and map to another person on their team who will then try to locate another cache site. Continue in this fashion until everyone on the team has gone out to get a cache marker (tape) or all 5 caches have been found. Record the time it takes each team to retrieve all 5 cache markers. Mark on the map where each cache was found.

Day Three will be just like day 2 but each team will take another team's control card and try to locate the caches from that section of the field. Each team member needs to mark the spot on the map where they found the cache. Record the times it takes each team to retrieve all 5 cache markers.

Calculate the two-day total to determine which team accomplished the task in the least amount of time.

The transition site should be at one location and the person on the team who is retrieving the control card should carry the card with them to the cache site. Each class will have their own set of maps and control cards which should be collected at the end of the period.

Lesson Four: Seek the Problem, Find the Solution

Level: grades 7+

Objectives:

1. Each task is designed so that a group must employ cooperation and some physical effort to gain a solution.

2. The group will develop decision making, leadership, and use both mental and physical strengths of a team.

3. The initiative problems will help to build morale and a sense of camaraderie.

Procedure:

4. Choose a problem suited to the age and physical ability of the group.

5. Find a safe and convenient place to set up the problem and make use of existing materials and supports whenever possible.

6. Make all the rules and procedures clear to the participants before they attempt the problem.

7. Be strict in administering the rules of the problem.

8. Set up the initiatives listed adding any of your own that you may like. For each initiative that is set up, record the location and waypoints on a master map. In a container at the site you will hide the description of the initiative, which explains the rules they must follow, along with any material that they need to perform the initiative.

9. Each group will be assigned a series of (4) numbers from the set in random order.

Initiative One:

T P Shuffle: Using the telephone pole that is lying on the ground have the group divide themselves evenly into 2 groups of about 8-10 students so that the two groups are facing each other in single file. The problem is for the 2 groups to exchange ends of the pole without touching the ground. Time the entire procedure giving a 15 second penalty any time anyone touches the ground. Record the group's time and place it in the container.

Initiative Two:

Trolley: The object of this initiative problem is to move your entire group (8-10) from a safe area over a designated poisonous plot to the far side using the props given. The trolleys are made up of two 4" by 4" pieces of wood of any length up to 16' long depending upon the size of the group. Drill 10 holes in each board in order to run a five foot long rope through or else use ten 10' jump ropes. The group must coordinate their steps to move across the designated area as quickly as possible without anyone falling off. Record the group's time and place it in the container.

Initiative Three:

Traffic Jam: The object of this problem is to have two groups of people (4 on each side) exchange places on a line of squares that has one more place than the number of people in both groups. The markers should be placed in easy step from one another. To begin, each group of 4 faces to the center unoccupied square. Using the following moves the people on the right side must end up on the left side, and vice versa.

Illegal Moves:

1. Any move backwards

2. Any move around someone facing the same way you are (their back is to you).

3. Any move which involves 2 persons moving at once.

Legal Moves

1. A person may move into an empty space in front of them.

2. A person may move around a person who is facing them into an empty space.

Record the time it takes to solve the problem and place it in the container.

Initiative Four:

Two by Four: Ask 8 people in the group to line up shoulder to shoulder facing one direction, alternating male/female (if possible). See if the group can end up with males on one side and females on the other side using the following rules:

1. The criterion is to complete the problem in the least amount of moves. Four moves is the minimum of moves. (do not announce this at first)

2. All moves must be made as pairs. Anyone next to you is a potential member of a pair, male or female.

3. As a pair moves, they leave an empty slot in the line which must remain and be eventually filled by another pair.

4. Pairs may not pivot or turn around.

5. The final line must be solid, i.e., no gaps.

Record the time it takes and place it in the container.

Back in the classroom have the students go over how they solved each of their initiatives. The details should be discussed by all involved. The discussion should focus on the process the students have just experienced. They can examine what decisions were made and by whom. The discussion can also focus on the roles of males and females and athletes and scholars, etc. Finally have them brainstorm to figure out ways that they could have done better. Time permitting you can let the groups try the tasks again to see if they can improve their times.

Lesson Five: Let's Play Ball

Objectives:

- The students will demonstrate their knowledge of the rules of various sports.

- The students will use a variety of strategies to estimate, compute, solve, and explain solutions to problems.

- The students will use the answers they compute to help them find the next set of questions.

Materials:

- GPS receivers

- Student map

- Field sheets

- Canisters to hold sports questions

- Control card with initial waypoint and code

Procedures:

- Set the course up within a confined area like a baseball field.

- Set canisters at 6 different waypoints. Each canister will contain 6 sports trivia questions numbered 1-6.

- Each group will be assigned a series of (5) numbers from the set in random order.

- Make up 6 different control cards and give each group a control card that has the starting waypoint and the code they are to follow: i.e.,N41*84.864 and W83*39.354 (site #3) 2, 4, 5, 1, and 6.

- When the group arrives at a cache they need to answer the sports trivia questions that are listed on their control card (#2). If they answer the questions and solve the problems correctly, they should come up with the new coordinates.

- At the next cache, there will be a similar set of questions that they need to solve that will lead them to the next one, and so on.

This is what a question in the cache may look like: Number of players on a soccer team multiplied by 12 (abc). N41*39.abc. Number of meters in a mile divided by 5 (def). W83*345.def. The new coordinates are: N41*39.132. W83*345.320

*Note for teachers: Mark out the coordinates that you will need to do the exercise and ask the questions in order to come out with the answer you need to fit the coordinates you have set.

Sample questions:

- #1. Number of players on a soccer team squared (ABC) and the number of minutes in a regulation HS game multiplied by 4 (DEF).

- #2. The second point in a tennis game multiplied by 10 (ABC) and the number of games you need to win in a set multiplied by the number of letters in the alphabet (DEF).

- #3. The number of yards to make a first down in football multiplied by the number of weeks in a year (ABC) and the length of the football field in meters (DEF)

- #4. The amount of fouls a basketball player can receive in a game multiplied by 12 dozen (ABC) and the amount of seconds in an eight minute quarter divided by 4 (DEF).

- #5. How many possible outs are there in a seven inning softball game added to 500 (ABC) and the distance in feet between the bases in softball multiplied by 4 (DEF).

- #6. The number of meters each runner runs in a 3200 meter relay (ABC) and the number of hurdles in a 400 meter race if they are spaced out every 20 meters. squared (DEF).

Lesson Six: Finding Perimeter

Level: Beginner

Objective:

Introduction to absolute locations

1. Measure side lengths, perimeter, and area of different playing fields.

2. Develop and use strategies to find perimeter using the GPS.

3. Draw and label the side lengths on a piece of graph paper.

Materials:

- GPS receiver
- Field sheets
- Graph paper
- Measuring tape
- Map of the field

Procedures:

1. Go out into the playing fields and mark out the waypoints for the perimeter of the playing field, i.e., the soccer field or football field. (Any geometric shape can be plotted out.)

2. Bring the class out to the playing field and have them investigate perimeters of the field based on the waypoints you gave them.

3. The group will go to each waypoint by setting the coordinates given to them by the teacher into the GPS.

4. Record the waypoints on the map of the field.

5. Write down the distance between points by using pacing (determine how long one stride is: It is usually about 1 meter) or measure the field using a large tape measure.

6. Record the distance between points on the master map.

Back in the Classroom:

Ask the students to draw their own diagram of the field on a piece of paper. Have them place the coordinates at the four corners of the field.

N 41* 32.**565**	B	N 41* 32.**565**
W 083* 35.**854**		W 083* 35.**791**
A		**C**
N 41* 32.**554**		N 41* 32.**554**
W 083* 35.**854**	D	W 083* 35.**791**

Based on the numbers in bold print can you tell which lines (A., B., C., or D.) were measured on the lines of latitude? The lines of longitude? Hint: Which numbers do not change?

Variations: Have the students find the perimeter of an irregular figure like the playground or the baseball field. Make them measure out the distance between points.

Scale and Distance

Maps are by necessity, drawn to scale and it is this scale, which determines the distance between points on the actual ground. There is still more knowledge that needs to be acquired on how to estimate distance, and this we will learn by "STEP-COUNTING". This is a very old technique of judging how far away things are. The Roman soldiers used this technique and counted 'double steps' in groups of 1000. This was called the 'mille passus' in Latin, and this is where the word mile came from and the actual distance. To practice 'step-counting' we will need to be in an area of at least 100 meters. We will need a 100 meter tape, some markers, paper, and pencil. These activities will help develop a sense of the relationship between distance on the map and the actual distance on the ground. The instructor marks out 100m on a field with a marker at each end. Using double pace counting, i.e., count each time the right or left foot hits the ground; participants carry out the following exercise:

Here is the practice

1. Walk the 100 meters and count every time the right foot comes to the ground. Write down the answer.

2. Walk back again, count, and write down the answer.

3. Repeat 1 and 2 again. Add these figures together and divide by 4 to obtain your personal step-count figure for walking 100 meters.

4. Repeat these same procedures, but this time run at a steady 'marathon' pace. The average figure you obtain this time will be your step-count figure for running 100 meters.

5. Try this same process but do it in rough terrain.

Points to note: Don't over-stride when walking and don't run 100 meters at a dash speed.

Exercise

Use the chart below to calculate your results.

Number of DOUBLE STEPS in 100 m

Walking	Open Space	Rough Terrain
Try 1		
Try 2		
Try 3		
Try 4		
Average		
Running	Open Space	Rough Terrain
Try 1		
Try 2		
Try 3		
Try 4		
Average		

WORK SHEETS

Geo-caching Work Sheet

Name(s): _____ Date: _____

Let's go Geo-caching! Lesson: Grand Slam

Student Name	Write the Waypoint Coordinates Start	Write the Waypoint Coordinates End	Distance Between Points
	N ____ ____ ____ W ____ ____ ____	N ____ ____ ____ W ____ ____ ____	
	N ____ ____ ____ W ____ ____ ____	N ____ ____ ____ W ____ ____ ____	
	N ____ ____ ____ W ____ ____ ____	N ____ ____ ____ W ____ ____ ____	
	N ____ ____ ____ W ____ ____ ____	N ____ ____ ____ W ____ ____ ____	
	N ____ ____ ____ W ____ ____ ____	N ____ ____ ____ W ____ ____ ____	
	N ____ ____ ____ W ____ ____ ____	N ____ ____ ____ W ____ ____ ____	

Back in the Classroom, based on the group distance; perform the calculations in the table below.

Farthest Kick	Shortest Kick	Group Mean	Group Median	Group Range

Geo-caching Work Sheet

Name(s): _____ Date: _____

Let's go Geo-caching! Lesson: Seek the Problem, Find the Solution

Initiative Number	Write the waypoint coordinates	Describe where you found the cache
	N ____ ____ ____ W ____ ____ ____	
	N ____ ____ ____ W ____ ____ ____	
	N ____ ____ ____ W ____ ____ ____	
	N ____ ____ ____ W ____ ____ ____	
	N ____ ____ ____ W ____ ____ ____	
	N ____ ____ ____ W ____ ____ ____	

Back In the Classroom

Be prepared to share the problem you found as well as the solution

Geo-caching Work Sheet

Name(s): _____ Date: _____

Let's go Geo-caching! Lesson: Let's Play Ball

Bring a calculator, pencil, control card, and a GPS receiver

Student Name	Code	Starting Waypoint	Second Waypoint	Third Waypoint	Fourth Waypoint	Fifth Waypoint	Sixth Waypoint
	1,5,6,2,4	N W	N W	N W	N W	N W	N W
	3,2,1,6,5	N W	N W	N W	N W	N W	N W
	4,3,5,1,2	N W	N W	N W	N W	N W	N W
	6,4,3,5,1	N W	N W	N W	N W	N W	N W
	5,6,2,4,3	N W	N W	N W	N W	N W	N W
	2,1,4,3,6	N W	N W	N W	N W	N W	N W

Assist the students as needed outside. Be aware that they may solve problems incorrectly, and therefore will not find the next container. In this case, encourage the group to go back to their last cache, read the problem again and check their work.

Geo-caching Work Sheet

Name(s): _____ Date: _____

Let's go Geo-caching! Lesson: Finding Perimeter

	Write the waypoint coordinates	Distance Between Points
Point A	N ____ ____ ____ W ____ ____ ____	
Point B	N ____ ____ ____ W ____ ____ ____	
Point C	N ____ ____ ____ W ____ ____ ____	
Point D	N ____ ____ ____ W ____ ____ ____	
Point E	N ____ ____ ____ W ____ ____ ____	
Point F	N ____ ____ ____ W ____ ____ ____	

Back In the Classroom

Be prepared to share the problem you found and to draw out your measurements and label the side lengths.

Interactive
Games

Coordinate Round Up

Objective: collect all the poly dots in sequence based on the coordinates found on the back of the poly dot so that the last dot picked up says Congratulations you WON!

Preparation: You will need 2 sets of poly dots (or more if large groups) numbered 1-30. Every dot will have a coordinate on the back of the dot which will tell you which dot to pick up next. For example: Start with the coordinate (5, 2) that will bring you to the # 11. On the back of the #11 dot will have the coordinate (2, 3) which goes to #14, on the back of #14 put (3, 5) which goes to #27. Keep numbering the dots with the next coordinate in the sequence until there is only one dot left. In this case it would be the #1 and on the back of that dot it would say WINNER!

Set Up

Start card has coordinates (5, 2)

25	26	27	28	29	30
(4,3)	(4,2)	(4,5)	(6,3)	(3,1)	(1,3)
19	20	21	22	23	24
(2,2)	(1,2)	(6,5)	(5,5)	(2,5)	(5,4)
13	14	15	16	17	18
(4,1)	(3,5)	(3,2)	(2,1)	(3,4)	(1,4)
7	8	9	10	11	12
(5,1)	(6,1)	(6,2)	(1,5)	(2,3)	(2,4)
1	2	3	4	5	6
(Winner!)	(1,1)	(3,3)	(4,4)	(6,4)	(5,3)

0, 0

The Sole Survivor

Objective: Be the last person left on the planet by using cunning and speed

Preparation: Set poly dots at each of the 4 cardinal directions (N, S, E, & W). Have the students stand at the equator and the prime meridian (0, 0). Tell the class where the locations are; what direction they need to go to get to N, S, E, or W. On your signal they are to run to the location announced and try to stand on a poly dot. Anyone who does not land on a dot is out of the game (this game is similar to musical chairs). Have everyone go back to the middle and take away a number of dots from each location. Call another direction and the students must move to the new location and stand on a poly dot. Again if you do not find a dot to stand on you are eliminated. Tell the students to go back to the middle and again take away dots. Keep going in this fashion until only 2 people are left and on the final call there will be a SOLE SURVIVOR!

Suggestion to teachers: take away more dots at the beginning of the game and when the number of survivors drops take away 1-2 dots.

You can play this game again using inter-cardinal directions (NE, NW, SE, and SW).

How Many Satellites?

Depending on how clear the day is, how open the area, whether you are in the mountains or surrounded by mountains, or various other obstacles or barriers that are around you, will play a role in navigation. How many satellites that we can acquire, will help in navigation.

Objective: Be the first person to call out how many satellites are orbiting around them.

Preparation: Have students find a partner. Using both hands on the signal (1, 2, 3, GO!) have the students put out 0-10 fingers and try to be the first person to add the number of fingers correctly. Play the game several times adding fingers and then try it by subtracting fingers from 20. How did they do?

Find Your Satellite

Each satellite has a unique signal that is transmitted to a GPS. The job of the GPS is to recognize that signal and follow it.

Objective: Be able to recognize similar sounds to locate the satellite that will direct you.

Preparation: Have students find a partner. Tell them to come up with a unique sound or word that will help them locate one another. Have the students move about the room far away from their partner. Instruct the students to put their hands up, palms facing out, and chest level to act as bumpers for safety. On your signal everyone is to close their eyes and begin making their sounds. Can you locate your partner using only satellite signals?

Secret Satellite

Satellites must triangulate to locate a position. Therefore depending upon the place or object you are trying to locate will depend on the satellites working together.

Objective: Locate the satellites that are directing you.

Preparation: Have the students form a large circle. Explain to the class that everyone is a satellite and they are responsible for giving communication signals to someone in the class. The only way to give the signal is to keep the receiver (student A) between you and some other student in the class who is your secret satellite. This is how satellites work by using Triangulation. To begin the game every student must pick someone as the receiver they are communicating with and someone who is to be their second satellite. A third invisible satellite is always with you to help in the triangulation. Do not tell anyone who you pick.

Rules: You must keep your receiver in between you and your second satellite at all times. Therefore as your receiver moves and your secret satellite moves you must move to always keep the triangulation working. Everyone will have a different secret satellite and a different receiver which leads to the FUN or CHAOS. Can you keep your receiver in a position to receive the signal from all 3 satellites?

Satellite Shuffle

Satellites are continuously working to help locate a position on earth. Numerous conditions and factors will affect the degree of accuracy of satellites. It may take up to a minute or more for the satellites to acquire an exact location. This activity represents how the satellites might hop from one location to another as it is trying to pick up the best signal.

Objective: See how satellites work to pick up the best signal and thus give an accurate location.

Preparation: Have the students get into groups of 4. They need to make a line where 1 person is the lead and 2 are in the middle and 1 person's at the end. Tell the students that when you give the following commands they are to move as directed. When you call out rotate everyone in the group turns around and faces the other direction. When you call out switch, the first person in line moves to the back of the line, and the last person in the line, moves to the front of the line. When you call change, the 2 people in the middle of the line change places. Everyone is to be moving at all times.

Snatch a Satellite

Have you ever entered in to the "Dead Zone"? How annoying it is to lose satellite reception. In this interactive game there are poly dots scattered around the ground. Each poly dot represents a spot where you get good satellite reception. The only problem is that there are not enough poly dots for people looking for satellite reception. Begin the game with as many people that can stand on a dot. There should be several people without a dot. On the whistle everyone must come off their dot and find a new dot. You may not go back to the same dot you were on for at least 3 switches forcing everyone to locate new dots and to prevent anyone from going back to the same dot time after time. No one is eliminated in this game but after several switches see how many people was not left in the "Dead Zone".

ABOUT THE AUTHOR

I am a teaching professional and I have been involved in implementing several new programs into the school curriculum. I use alternative lessons that include a series of hands-on activities, worksheets, and interactive games getting the students up and active. The activities are fun and educational promoting individual thinking through problem solving and exploration. Most of the activities can be used at any grade level and they are multi-disciplinary. Each lesson is created to encourage cooperation, problem solving, and decision making. Over the years I have had numerous opportunities to try new programs and make the necessary adjustments or changes in order to make an activity that is fun and challenging. I am always interested in new challenges and because of this I try to bring this same enthusiasm for adventure to the classroom.